ASEAN ECONOMIC COOPERATION AND INTEGRATION

ASEAN economic cooperation and integration have come a long way since the organisation's early days, when cooperation was more political and diplomatic than economic in nature. ASEAN now constitutes the most ambitious organisation of regional cooperation and integration in the developing world. This book investigates the economics of various ASEAN and ASEAN-centric economic integration initiatives, focusing in particular on the ASEAN Economic Community (AEC). In addition to assessing the potential effects of the AEC on the economies of the ten ASEAN member states via changes in trade, foreign direct investment and economic structure, this book underscores the implementation challenges ASEAN faces as it completes the AEC project. It also considers the AEC in the context of the Regional Comprehensive Economic Partnership (RCEP). This comprehensive study is written for academic researchers and students, as well as for policy makers in ASEAN as they chart the future policy path of the region.

SIOW YUE CHIA is Senior Research Fellow at the Singapore Institute of International Affairs. Previously, Dr Chia was Executive Director of the Institute of Southeast Asian Studies (Singapore), founding Regional Coordinator of the East Asian Development Network (EADN), and Economics Professor at the National University of Singapore. She has consulted for international, regional and Singapore organisations such as the World Bank,

WTO and Asian Development Bank. Her research and publications cover international trade and investment, international labour mobility, and regional economic integration, with focus on the Asia Pacific, East Asia, Southeast Asia and Singapore.

MICHAEL G. PLUMMER is Director of SAIS Europe and the Eni Professor of International Economics at the Johns Hopkins University. He was until recently Head of the Development Division of the OECD and was Associate Professor of Economics at Brandeis University before coming to SAIS. He has worked on numerous projects for international organisations, development and other government agencies, and regional development banks. His main academic interests relate to international trade, international finance, and Asian economic integration, especially in the ASEAN context.

INTEGRATION THROUGH LAW

The Role of Law and the Rule of Law in ASEAN Integration

General Editors

J. H. H. Weiler, European University Institute
Tan Hsien-Li, National University of Singapore
Michael Ewing-Chow, National University of Singapore

The Association of Southeast Asian Nations (ASEAN), comprising the ten member states of Brunei Darussalam, Cambodia, Indonesia, Lao PDR, Malaysia, Myanmar, Philippines, Singapore, Thailand and Vietnam, has undertaken intensified integration into the ASEAN Community through the Rule of Law and Institutions in its 2007 Charter. This innovative book series evaluates the community-building processes of ASEAN to date and offers a conceptual and policy toolkit for broader Asian thinking and planning of different legal and institutional models of economic and political regional integration in the region. Participating scholars have been divided up into six separate thematic strands. The books combine a mix of Asian and Western scholars.

Centre for International Law, National University of Singapore (CIL-NUS)

The Centre for International Law (CIL) was established in 2009 at the National University of Singapore's Bukit Timah Campus in response to the growing need for international law expertise and capacity building in the Asia-Pacific region. CIL is a university-wide research centre that focuses on multidisciplinary research and works with other NUS or external centres of research and academic excellence. In particular, CIL collaborates very closely with the NUS Faculty of Law.

INTEGRATION THROUGH LAW
The Role of Law and the Rule of Law in ASEAN Integration
General Editors: J. H. H. Weiler, Tan Hsien-Li and Michael Ewing-Chow

ASEAN ECONOMIC COOPERATION AND INTEGRATION

Progress, Challenges and Future Directions

SIOW YUE CHIA AND
MICHAEL G. PLUMMER

CAMBRIDGE
UNIVERSITY PRESS

CAMBRIDGE
UNIVERSITY PRESS

University Printing House, Cambridge CB2 8BS, United Kingdom

Cambridge University Press is part of the University of Cambridge.

It furthers the University's mission by disseminating knowledge in the pursuit of education, learning and research at the highest international levels of excellence.

www.cambridge.org
Information on this title: www.cambridge.org/9781107503878

First published 2015

A catalogue record for this publication is available from the British Library

ISBN 978-1-107-50387-8 Paperback

CONTENTS

FIGURES

TABLES

GENERAL EDITORS' PREFACE

This monograph is published within the context of a wide-ranging research project entitled, Integration Through Law: The Role of Law and the Rule of Law in ASEAN Integration (ITL), undertaken by the Centre for International Law at the National University of Singapore and directed by J. H. H. Weiler, Michael Ewing-Chow and Tan Hsien-Li.

The Preamble to the ASEAN Charter concludes with a single decision: "We, the Peoples of the Member States of the Association of Southeast Asian Nations ... [h]ereby decide to establish, through this Charter, the legal and institutional framework for ASEAN." For the first time in its history of over four decades, the Legal and the Institutional were brought to the forefront of ASEAN discourse.

The gravitas of the medium, a Charter: the substantive ambition of its content, the creation of three interlocking Communities, and the turn to law and institutions as instruments for realization provide ample justification for this wide-ranging project, to which this monograph is one contribution, examining ASEAN in a comparative context.

That same substantive and, indeed, political ambition means that any single study, illuminating as it may be, will cover but a fraction of the phenomena. Our modus operandi in this project was to create teams of researchers from Asia and elsewhere who would contribute individual monographs within an overall framework which we had designed. The project framework, involving several thematic clusters within each monograph, is thus determined by the framework and the place of each monograph within it.

As regards the specific content, however, the authors were free, indeed encouraged, to define their own understanding of the problem and their own methodology and reach their own conclusions. The thematic structure of the entire project may be found at the end of this Preface.

The project as a whole, and each monograph within it, display several methodological sensibilities.

First, law, in our view, can only be understood and evaluated when situated in its political and economic context. Thus, the first studies in the overall project design are intended to provide the political, economic, cultural and historical context against which one must understand ASEAN and are written by specialists in these respective disciplines. This context, to a greater or lesser degree, also informs the sensibility of each monograph. There are no "black letter law" studies to be found in this project and, indeed, even in the most technical of areas we encouraged our authors to make their writing accessible to readers of diverse disciplines.

Comparative experience suggests that the success of achieving some of the more ambitious objectives outlined in Article 1 of the Charter will depend in no small measure on the effectiveness of legal principles, legal rules and legal institutions. This is particularly true as regards the success of establishing "an ASEAN Community comprising the ASEAN Security Community, the ASEAN Economic Community and the ASEAN Socio-Cultural Community as provided for in the Bali Declaration of ASEAN Concord II". Article 2(2)(n) stipulates the commitment of ASEAN Member States to act in accordance with the principle of "adherence to multilateral trade rules and ASEAN's rules-based regimes for effective implementation of economic commitments and progressive reduction towards elimination of all barriers to regional economic integration." The ASEAN Member States therefore envisage that rules of law and the Rule of Law will become a major feature in the future of ASEAN.

Although, as seen, the Charter understands itself as providing an institutional and legal framework for ASEAN, the question of the "role of law and the rule of law" is not advocacy but a genuine enquiry in the various substantive areas of the project as to:

- the substantive legal principles and substantive rules of the various ASEAN communities;
- the procedural legal principles and rules governing institutional structures and decision-making processes;
- implementation, enforcement and dispute settlement.

One should not expect a mechanical application of this scheme in each study; rather, a sensibility that refuses to content itself with legal enactments as such and looks to a "living" notion of law and institutions is ubiquitous in all the studies. Likewise, the project is sensitive to "non Law." It variously attempts to locate the appropriate province of the law in this experience. That is, not only the role of law, but also the areas that are and should remain outside the reach of legal institutionalization with due sensitivity to ASEAN and Asian particularism and political and cultural identities.

The project, and the monographs of which it is made, are not normatively thick. They do not advocate. They are designed, for the most part, to offer reflection, discuss the pros and cons, and in this way enrich public awareness, deepen understanding of different options and in that respect contribute indirectly to policymaking.

This decisive development of ASEAN has been accompanied by a growing Asian interest in various legal and institutional forms of transnational economic and political cooperation, notably the various voices discussing and showing an interest in an East Asia Integration project. The number of Free Trade Agreements (FTAs) and Regional Trade Agreements (RTAs) has increased from six in 1991 to 166 in 2013, with a further 62 in various stages of negotiations.

Methodologically, the project and many of the monographs are comparative in their orientation. Comparative law is one of the few real-life laboratories that we have in which to assess and understand the operation of different legal and institutional models designed to tackle similar objectives and problems. One should not need to put one's own hand in the fire to learn that it scorches. With that in mind a couple of monographs offer both conceptual reflection and pragmatic "tool boxing" on some of the key elements featuring in all regional integration systems.

Comparative law is in part about divergence: it is a potent tool and means to understand one's own uniqueness. One understands better the uniqueness of Apples by comparing them to Oranges. You understand better the specialness of a Toyota by comparing it to a Ford.

Comparative law is also about convergence: it is a potent tool and means to understand how what are seemingly different phenomena are part of a broader trend, an insight which may enhance both self-understanding and policy potentialities.

Although many studies in the project could have almost immediate policy implications, as would the project as a whole, this is not its only or even principal purpose. There is a rich theory of federalism which covers many countries around the world. There is an equally rich theory of European integration, which has been associated with the advent Union. There is also considerable learning on Free Trade Areas and the like.

To date, the study of the legal aspects of ASEAN specifically and other forms of Asian legal integration has been derivative of, and dependent on, theoretical and conceptual insight which were developed in different contexts.

One principal objective of ITL and these monographs will be to put in place the building blocks for an authentic body of ASEAN and Asian integration theory developed in, and with sensitivity to, the particularities and peculiarities of the region and continent. A theory and conceptual framework of Asian legal integration will signal the coming of age of research of and in the region itself.

Although the monographs form part of an overarching project, we asked our authors to write each as a "standalone" – not assuming that their readers would have consulted any of the other titles. Indeed, the project is rich and few will read all monographs. We encourage readers to pick and choose from the various monographs and design their own menu. There is, on occasion, some overlap in providing, for example, background information on ASEAN in different studies. That is not only inevitable but desirable in a project of this amplitude.

The world is increasingly witnessing a phenomenon of interlocking regional organization where the experience of one feeds on the others. In some way, the intellectual, disciplinary and comparative sensibility of this project is a microcosm of the world it describes.

The range of topics covered in this series comprises:

The General Architecture and Aspirations of ASEAN
The Governance and Management of ASEAN: Instruments, Institutions, Monitoring, Compliance and Dispute Resolution
Legal Regimes in ASEAN
The ASEAN Economic Community
ASEAN and the World
The Substantive Law of ASEAN

ABBREVIATIONS

AANZFTA	ASEAN–Australia–New Zealand Free Trade Area
ABMI	Asian Bond Market Initiative
ACIA	ASEAN Comprehensive Investment Area
ACCSQ	ASEAN Consultative Committee for Standards and Quality
ACFTA	ASEAN–China FTA
ACMF	ASEAN Capital Market Forum
ADB	Asian Development Bank
AEC	ASEAN Economic Community
AEMM	ASEAN Economic Ministers' Meeting
AFAFGIT	ASEAN Framework Agreement on the Facilitation of Goods in Transit
AFAS	ASEAN Framework Agreement on Services
AFC	Asian Financial Crisis
AFMM	ASEAN Finance Ministers' Meeting
AFTA	ASEAN Free Trade Area
AHTN	ASEAN Harmonised Tariff Nomenclature
AIA	ASEAN Investment Area
AIC	ASEAN Industrial Complementation
AICO	ASEAN Industrial Cooperation
AIF	ASEAN Infrastructure Fund
AIFS	ASEAN Integrated Food Security
AIFTA	ASEAN–India Free Trade Area

AIJV	ASEAN Industrial Joint Venture
AIMO	ASEAN Integration Monitoring Office
AIP	ASEAN Industrial Project
AJCEP	ASEAN–Japan Comprehensive Economic Partnership
AKFTA	ASEAN–Korea Free Trade Area
AMBDC	ASEAN Mekong Basin Development Cooperation
APAEC	ASEAN Plan of Action on Energy Cooperation
APSC	ASEAN Political-Security Community
APT	ASEAN Plus Three
APTERR	ASEAN Plus Three Emergency Rice Reserve
APTCS-FSBD	APT Comprehensive Strategy on Food Security and Bio-energy Development
ASCC	ASEAN Socio-Cultural Community
ASEAN	Association of Southeast Asian Nations
ASEAN+3	ASEAN + China, Japan and South Korea
ASEAN+6	ASEAN+3 (+ India, Australia and New Zealand)
ASEAN5	Original ASEAN Members (Indonesia, Malaysia, the Philippines, Thailand and Singapore)
ASEAN6	Indonesia, Malaysia, the Philippines, Singapore, Thailand and Brunei, Darussalam
ASEAN10	Brunei Darussalam, Cambodia, Indonesia, Laos, Malaysia, Myanmar, the Philippines, Singapore, Thailand, Viet Nam
ASEAN PTA	ASEAN Preferential Trading Arrangement

ASSM	ASEAN Single Shipping Market
ASW	ASEAN Single Window
ATIGA	ASEAN Trade in Goods Agreement
B-to-B	brand-to-brand
CEPEA	Comprehensive Economic Partnership for East Asia
CEPT	Common Effective Preferential Tariff
CET	Common External Tariff
CGE	Computable General Equilibrium
CGIF	Credit Guarantee and Investment Facility
CLMV	Cambodia, Lao People's Democratic Republic, Myanmar and Vietnam
CMIM	Chiang Mai Initiative Multilateralised
CTC	change in tariff classification
CTH	change in tariff heading
CTSH	change in tariff sub-heading
CU	customs union
EAFTA	East Asia Free Trade Area
EEC	European Economic Community
EED	Equitable Economic Development
EU	European Union
FDI	foreign direct investment
FTA	free trade agreement
GATS	General Agreement on Trade in Services
GEL	General Exclusion List
GFC	global financial crisis
GNI	gross national income
GNI-PPP	gross national income based on purchasing-power parity
HDI	Human Development Index

HLTF	High Level Task Force
HSL	highly sensitive list
IAI	Initiative for ASEAN Integration
ICT	information and communication technology
IL	inclusion list
IPR	intellectual property rights
IT	information technology
LPI	Logistics Performance Index
MAAFS	Multilateral Agreement on the Full Liberalisation of Air Freight Services
MFA	Multi-Fibre Arrangement
MFN	most-favoured nation
MNC	multinational corporation
MNP	Movement of Natural Persons
MRA	mutual recognition arrangement
NAFTA	North American Free Trade Area
NSW	national single window
NTB	non-tariff barrier
NTM	non-tariff measure
OECD	Organisation for Economic Co-operation and Development
PIS	priority integration sector
ppp	purchasing-power parity
PTA	Preferential Trade Arrangement
QR	quantitative restriction
RCEP	Regional Comprehensive Economic Partnership
ROO	rules of origin
RVC	regional value content

SL	sensitive list
SME	small and medium-sized enterprise
SOE	state-owned enterprise
SPCD	Strategic Plan of Customs Development
TEL	temporary exclusion list
TPP	Trans-Pacific Partnership
UNIDO	United Nations Industrial Development Organization
VAP	Vientiane Action Programme
WTO	World Trade Organization

Chapter 1

Introduction

The 1967 Bangkok Declaration established the Association of Southeast Asian Nations (ASEAN) by the five founding members of Indonesia, Malaysia, the Philippines, Singapore and Thailand. ASEAN was joined by Brunei (hereafter collectively referred to as the ASEAN6) in 1984 and by Cambodia, Laos, Myanmar and Vietnam (hereafter collectively referred to as CLMV) in 1995–9. The two-page ASEAN Declaration contains the aims and purposes of the Association, which include cooperation in the economic, social, cultural, technical, educational and other fields, the promotion of regional peace and stability through abiding respect for justice and the rule of law, and adherence to the principles of the United Nations Charter. The initial objective of ASEAN was to prevent regional conflicts, build mutual confidence and promote regional stability and security so as to lay the regional foundation for the pursuit of economic development. Reference to economic cooperation was partly to dispel suspicions of ASEAN being a military alliance. It is to be noted that in the early years only ASEAN foreign ministers met regularly.

A new era of economic cooperation and integration began with the first ASEAN Summit of heads of state in 1976,

The authors would like to thank Ms Alissa Tafti and Ms Jenna Allen for excellent research assistance. They also profited from comments by two anonymous external referees.

followed by meetings of economic ministers. Economic cooperation schemes began in 1977 with the ASEAN Preferential Trading Arrangement (ASEAN PTA), followed by several industrial cooperation schemes. In 1992, in response to a rapidly changing global economic and strategic environment, ASEAN took the first serious step towards economic integration with the agreement on the ASEAN Free Trade Area (AFTA). This was followed in 1995 by the ASEAN Framework Agreement on Services (AFAS), and in 1998 by the agreement on the ASEAN Investment Area (AIA).

It should be recalled that in 1992 India was still mostly an inward-looking, poor country dealing with a major financial crisis and China was growing but still a relatively minor player in international markets. Neither country featured in the World Bank's 1993 *East Asian Miracle* study on 'high performing Asian economies'. However, two decades later, global competition has been intensifying, China and India have become formidable competitors as well as partners of ASEAN member states, successes at the multilateral Doha Development Agenda negotiations (started in November 2001) have been minimal,[1] and bilateral and regional preferential trading arrangements have proliferated. ASEAN has free trade agreements (FTAs) with the major trading partners of Japan, China, South Korea, India and Australia–New

[1] At the Ninth WTO Ministerial in Bali, 3–6 December 2013, the WTO member states did agree to a 'mini-package' that included aspects of trade facilitations, agriculture and development, showing that the Doha Development Agenda is still moving forward. However, much remains to be done in terms of the 'single undertaking'.

Zealand (and is negotiating with the European Union (or EU), but not with the USA), while individual ASEAN member states have numerous FTAs with partners throughout the world, including the USA and the EU.

It is against this backdrop that ASEAN leaders decided in 2003 to create the ASEAN Economic Community (AEC), complemented by the ASEAN Political-Security Community (APSC) and the ASEAN Socio-Cultural Community (ASCC). The AEC would create a single market and production base by 2020 (later advanced to 2015) via a free flow of goods, services, foreign direct investment (FDI), skilled labour and a freer flow of capital. It is a highly ambitious programme for economic integration.

Economic integration in ASEAN is arguably pressured more by perceptions of external 'threats' than internal conviction of the benefits of deeper intra-regional cooperation. The perceived external 'threat' to ASEAN's export market access and attractiveness for FDI with the formation of the North American Free Trade Area (NAFTA) and the European single market led to the decision to establish AFTA, AFAS and AIA in the 1990s. A subsequent perceived external 'threat' from the economic rise of China and India led to the 2003 decision to form the AEC.

This book examines the evolution of economic cooperation and integration from ASEAN's inception in 1967, highlighting progress and shortcomings, and suggesting possible next steps. Chapter 2 provides a brief overview of economic growth and trends in internationalisation in the ASEAN region. Chapter 3 examines trends in ASEAN's international trade and FDI and the role of commercial policy reforms and production networks. Chapter 4 analyses the rationale, process and challenges of institutionalised economic integration. Chapter 5 offers an overview of the components of the AEC and its implementation and assesses the economic effects that can be expected from its successful implementation. Chapter 6 examines the direction of ASEAN economic integration beyond AEC 2015.[2]

[2] The book benefits from the publication of former ASEAN Secretary General Severino which gives an 'insider' perspective of ASEAN leadership thinking, and the rationale and processes of ASEAN economic cooperation and integration (Severino 2006).

Chapter 2

ASEAN diversity, economic growth and internationalisation

2.1 ASEAN's economic diversity

ASEAN diversity has often been cited to explain difficulties in reaching consensus on the speed and depth of ASEAN economic integration. Table 2.1 below highlights the economic diversity as proxied by population size, GDP, per capita GDP and per capita GNI-PPP, trade openness and FDI dependence as of 2012. Vast differences continue to exist notwithstanding decades of economic cooperation and integration. Singapore and Brunei have high per capita incomes that better many in the Organisation for Economic Co-operation and Development (OECD), while Cambodia, Laos and Myanmar are the least developed economies.[1] Indonesia is ASEAN's largest economy, followed by Thailand and Malaysia, while, in comparison, Brunei, Cambodia, Laos and Myanmar are small economies. The diversities are reflected in the different production and export structures and commercial policies.

[1] In addition, and not shown in the table, is the diversity in natural resource endowment and financial resources. Several ASEAN countries are rich in oil and gas, mineral deposits, agricultural and marine resources and hydro power. Only Singapore is natural resource poor, but it has compensated for this by building up its financial reserves and human capital.

Table 2.1 *ASEAN: differences in size, level of development and trade and foreign direct investment dependence, 2012*

	Brunei	Indonesia	Malaysia	Philippines	Singapore	Thailand	Cambodia	Laos	Myanmar	Vietnam
Population (million)	0.4	246.9	29.2	96.7	5.3	66.8	14.9	6.6	52.8	90.7
Land area (thousand sq. km)	5.8	1,860.4	330.3	300	0.7	513.1	181	236.8	676.6	331.1
GDP (US$ billion)	16.6	878.4	303.5	250.3	270.5	390.9	14.2	9.2	57.8	140.6
GDP per capita (US$)	39,418	3,589	10,350	2,594	51,455	5,592	978	1,442	1,186	1,567
GDP per capita (ppp-adjusted)	52,059	4,736	15,955	4,289	60,744	8,907	2,287	2,825	1,393	3,440
Merchandise trade (US$ billion)	15.9	368	415.1	107.9	818.2	443.9	14	4.4	16	218.3
Trade/GDP ratio (%)	95.5	41.4	136.8	43.1	302.5	113.6	98.7	47.8	27.6	155.3
Inward foreign direct investment stock (US$ billion)	13.3	205.7	132.4	31	682.4	159.1	8.4	2.5	11.9	72.5
Inward foreign direct investment stock/ GDP ratio (%)	80.4	23.4	43.6	12.4	252.3	40.7	59.4	27	20.6	51.6

Note: GDP per capita, ppp-adjusted values are for 2011. Brunei population is for 2010; all other population values are estimates for 2012.
Source: Compiled from ASEAN Secretariat database, UNCTAD and UNCTAD World Investment Report 2013.

All ASEAN countries have become highly open trade economies, although there remains wide inter-country variation, with Singapore having the highest trade/GDP ratio and Myanmar and Indonesia the lowest. Generally smaller economies are more trade dependent than the very large ones. A high trade/GDP ratio may reflect competitiveness in the international market place, but also renders the economy highly vulnerable to business cycle fluctuations in international demand. There are also wide inter-country differences in investment regimes. The inward FDI stock is very unevenly spread among ASEAN countries, with Singapore the major recipient of inward FDI into manufacturing and services, while CLMV accounted for only a minor share of total ASEAN inward FDI stock.

Table 2.2 shows the wide diversity in competitiveness as proxied by rankings in the World Bank's 2014 'ease of doing business' index. Generally, Singapore stands at the top while CLMV is at the other end of the competitiveness spectrum. The rankings of the specific components of the index give an indication of the specific areas in which individual countries need to improve on their competitiveness. For example, it costs on average US$460 to export a container from Singapore but over four times as much (US$1,950) from Laos.

Wide differences among ASEAN countries in levels of development and, more particularly, in competitiveness and economic openness have affected ASEAN consensus building, speed of economic liberalisation and implementation of specific measures. In the early years of ASEAN, there was more economic competition than complementarity among its six members, as geographical and technological

Table 2.2 *Ranks of ASEAN economies in World Bank '"Doing Business" Report', 2014*

	Brunei	Cambodia	Indonesia	Laos	Malaysia	Myanmar	Philippines	Singapore	Thailand	Vietnam
Ease of doing business	59	137	120	159	6	182	108	1	18	99
Starting a business	137	184	175	85	16	189	170	3	91	109
Dealing with construction permits	46	161	88	96	43	150	99	3	14	29
Getting electricity	29	134	121	140	21	126	33	6	12	156
Registering property	116	118	101	76	35	154	121	28	29	51
Getting credit	55	42	86	159	1	170	86	3	73	42
Protecting investors	115	80	52	187	4	182	128	2	12	157
Paying taxes	20	65	137	119	36	107	131	5	70	149
Trading across borders	39	114	54	161	5	113	42	1	24	65
Documents to export (number)	5	8	4	10	4	9	6	3	5	5

Time to export (days)	19	22	17	23	11	25	15	6	14	21
Cost to export (US$ per container)	705	795	615	1,950	450	670	585	460	595	610
Documents to import (number)	5	9	8	10	4	9	7	3	5	8
Time to import (days)	15	24	23	26	8	27	14	4	13	21
Cost to import (US$ per container)	770	930	660	1,910	485	660	660	440	760	600
Enforcing contracts	161	162	147	104	30	188	114	12	22	46
Resolving Insolvency	48	163	144	189	42	155	100	4	58	149

Source: World Bank, *Doing Business 2014: Understanding Regulations for Small and Medium-Size Enterprises* (Washington, DC: World Bank, 2013): www.doingbusiness.org/~/media/GIAWB/Doing%20Business/Documents/Annual-reports/English/DB14-Full-Report.pdf.

similarities led to similar exports of natural resources and labour-intensive manufactures, both having to seek extra-ASEAN markets. However, since the mid-1980s, ASEAN economies were able to leverage their differences in endowment and cost structures to attract inward FDI and so participate in global and regional production networks and intra-industry trade. As a result, the ASEAN economies have become much more complementary, with growing intra-industry trade in parts and components.

2.2 ASEAN economic growth and internationalisation

Economic growth in ASEAN has been impressive in recent decades. Figures 2.1a and 2.1b show annual real GDP growth rates for the ASEAN6, CLMV and an ASEAN10 (that is, ASEAN6 and CLMV) aggregate for the period 1990–2012. Some member states, such as Singapore, Malaysia and Thailand, have experienced among the fastest growth rates in the world, and since the Asian Financial Crisis (AFC) of 1997–8 CLMV have done generally better than the ASEAN average, signalling the beginnings of economic convergence. This growth has not been monotonic: the AFC severely affected several ASEAN economies, and the 'twin shocks' of the USA-originated financial crisis of 2008–9 and the Eurozone debt crisis beginning in 2010 have taken their tolls on the region's growth performance, though there was a growth rebound in 2012 from 2010 to 2011.

A few points are worth noting. First, while there continues to be a good deal of variable economic performance

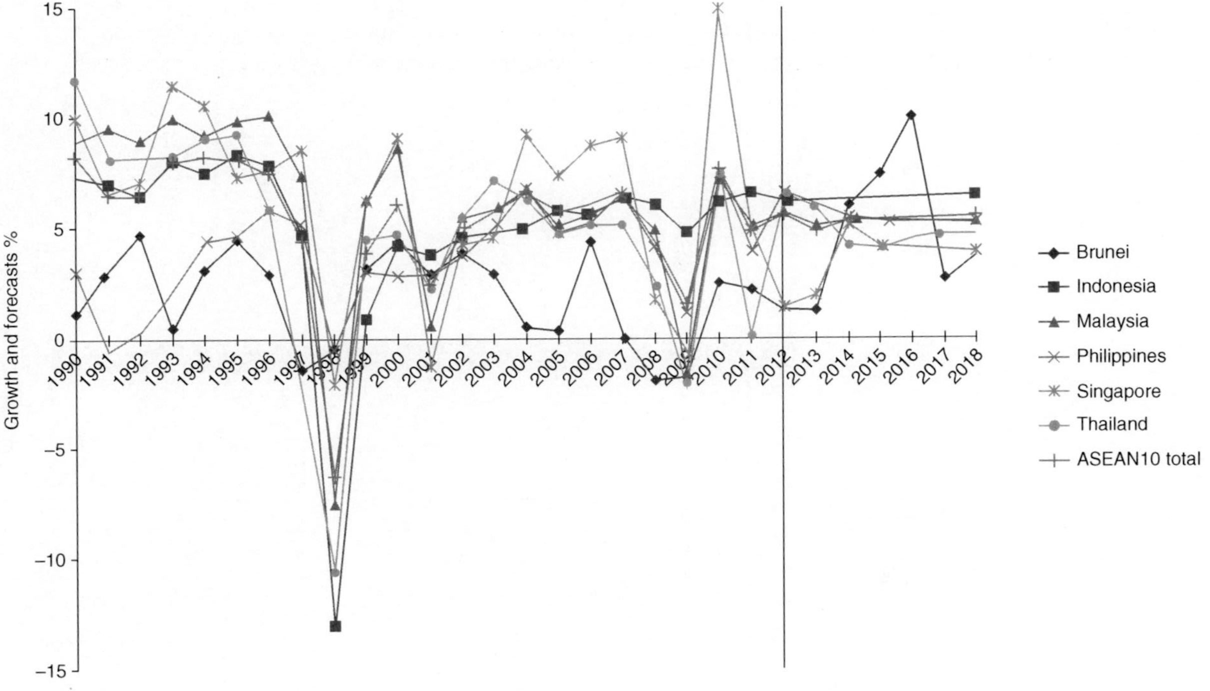

Figure 2.1a ASEAN GDP growth, 1990–2012 and forecasts, 2013–18 (Brunei, Indonesia, Malaysia, the Philippines, Singapore, Thailand)

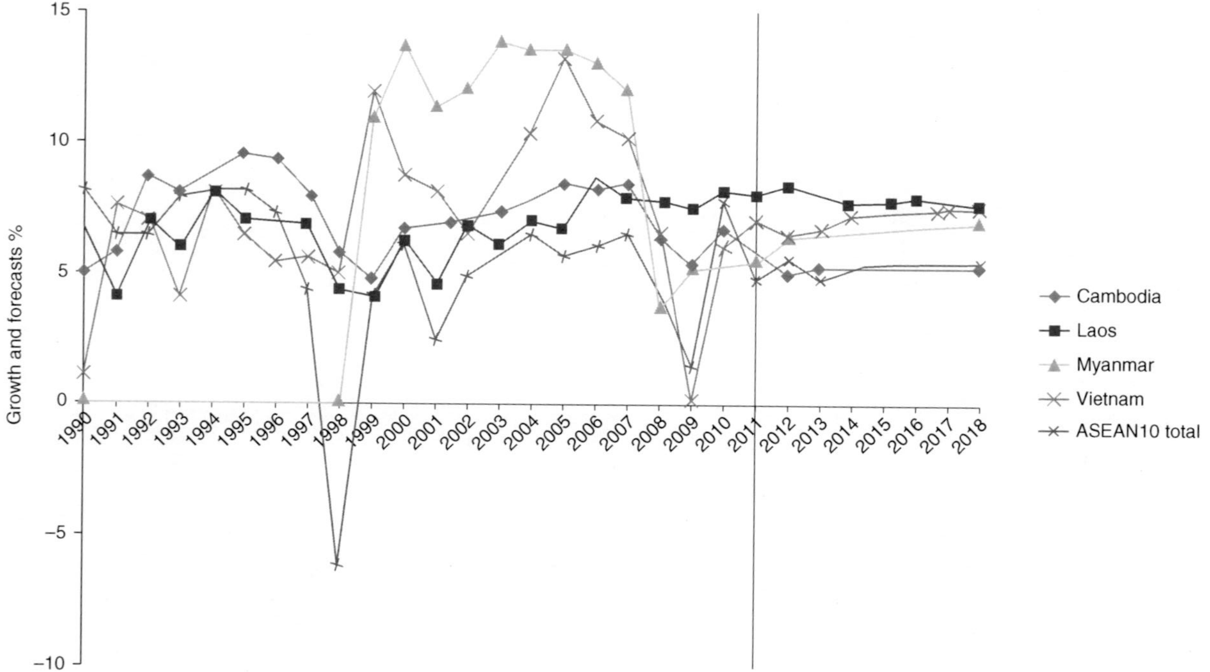

Figure 2.1b ASEAN GDP growth, 1990–2012 and forecasts, 2013–18 (Cambodia, Laos, Myanmar, Vietnam)
Source: IMF, World Economic Outlook Database: www.imf.org/external/pubs/ft/weo/2013/02/weodata/index.aspx.

among the ASEAN countries, growth rates themselves have been increasingly correlated since the AFC.[2] Important factors include the concerted economic reforms in the region and 'fragmented trade' in Asia with a rising degree of intra-industry trade.[3] Intra-industry trade constitutes over half of trade with Asia for Singapore, Thailand and Malaysia, and between one-third and two-fifths of the Indonesian and Philippine shares.[4] These figures are significantly up from just a decade ago, when no country's share was larger than about one-third. Second, while economic growth in any country is a complicated process, an important reason why ASEAN has excelled is its embrace of an outward-oriented development strategy. This has led to economic reforms that have facilitated the flow of factors of production across sectors in such a way as to reduce the costs of economic transition and permit an efficient reallocation of resources. Third, exports as a percentage of GDP, an indication of the internationalisation of an economy, have been rising in all ASEAN economies; for ASEAN as a whole, exports/GDP reached 61 per cent in 2010,

[2] See Asian Development Bank 2008: ch. 3 for a survey of these determinants as well as details on the convergence process.

[3] Intra-industry trade refers to exports and imports in the same industry (e.g., electronics for electronics) as opposed to inter-industry trade, which deals with trade across industries (e.g., oil for automobiles). With production networks and value chains, discussed at length below and in other chapters, trade across countries is increasingly intra-industry: for example, value added across an international electronics production chain will involve countries exchanging electronic components as they build their final good.

[4] See Rana 2008.

up from just 28 per cent in 1984.[5] This is a phenomenal increase in itself and relative to the rest of the world. In contrast, China and India had respective export/GDP shares in 2010 of 27 per cent and 13 per cent. At the country level, trade/GDP was above 40 per cent in all economies save Myanmar (Table 2.1).

While ASEAN's outward-orientation has served it well, its high dependence on external demand has also rendered its economies vulnerable to external shocks. Prior to the AFC, the ASEAN6 achieved a rate of growth that was significantly higher than its post-AFC trend. Productivity growth was driven by trade in those years, but domestic demand was far more important than international demand. After the AFC, growth has been driven more by external demand, with some countries registering large and persistent trade surpluses. Many ASEAN countries have been hit very hard by the USA and EU twin crises via the trade channel. For example, Singapore's growth performance has demonstrated the greatest volatility in recent years.[6] The focus of ASEAN leaders has rightly been on the need to reduce the region's *over-reliance* on external demand from the USA and EU, rather than turn the clock back on the internationalisation process.

5 For 2010 figures, see WTO Tariff Profiles, April 2012: http://stat.wto.org/TariffProfile/WSDBtariffPFExportZip.aspx?Language=E. For 1984 figures, see Plummer 2006.

6 Singapore's GDP growth rates were 8.9 per cent in 2007, 1.7 per cent in 2008, −1 per cent in 2009, 14.8 per cent in 2010, 5.3 per cent in 2011 and 1.3 per cent in 2012.

Chapter 3

ASEAN's international trade and foreign direct investment, commercial policy reforms and production networks

3.1 ASEAN's international trade in goods

ASEAN's approach to economic cooperation and integration focuses on the need to reduce barriers to intra-regional trade and investment so as to compete more effectively in international markets. What is needed is a more competitive regional economy in the context of an increasingly competitive global one. This makes ASEAN unique compared with economic integration efforts elsewhere, such as in the EU and Latin America, where the focus has been more on increasing intra-regional trade and investment as a percentage of the total.

Figure 3.1 shows that intra-ASEAN trade as a percentage of its total trade has remained fairly constant in the range of one-fifth to one-fourth over the past decade (2001–12), when economic integration programmes began to be implemented in earnest. In contrast, ASEAN's trade with China has almost tripled from 5 per cent to 13 per cent from 2001 to 2012, reflecting in large part the rising participation in regional production networks (particularly in electronics) along with China. China's rising importance has come at the expense of the traditional US and European markets, whose share fell from about one-third to one-fourth, and Japan. Note,

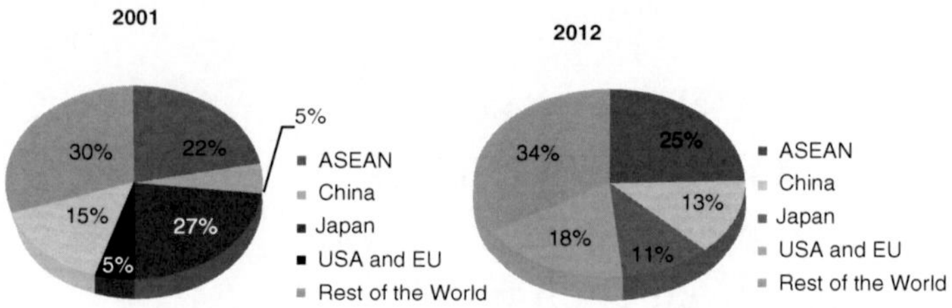

Figure 3.1 Direction of ASEAN trade, 2001 and 2012
Source: IMF, Direction of Trade Statistics: http://www.elibrary.imf.org.

however, that ASEAN is still dependent on these traditional OECD markets for the exports of final goods, when intermediate trade is separated from final demand in the trade data (see, for example, ADB 2008).[1]

At the country level, the importance of the ASEAN market varies considerably from economy to economy, as shown in Figures 3.2a and 3.2b. Laos and Myanmar are highly dependent on trade with ASEAN, as has been

[1] Analysis of international trade tends to focus on nominal values, which could be highly misleading. Value-added accounting (that is, export value less its import content) would be far more useful but is extremely difficult to do for lack of data. For example, Singapore's exports exceed its GDP in value, but would be much less when the import content of such exports are subtracted. The WTO and OECD have partnered in a project to decompose trade by value added, called TiVA (trade in value added). Likewise, focusing on bilateral trade balances could also be misleading. For example, in the USA–China dispute on bilateral trade balances China has argued that its exports to the USA are usually the products of American multinationals in China; thus, in a way, they are also of US origin.

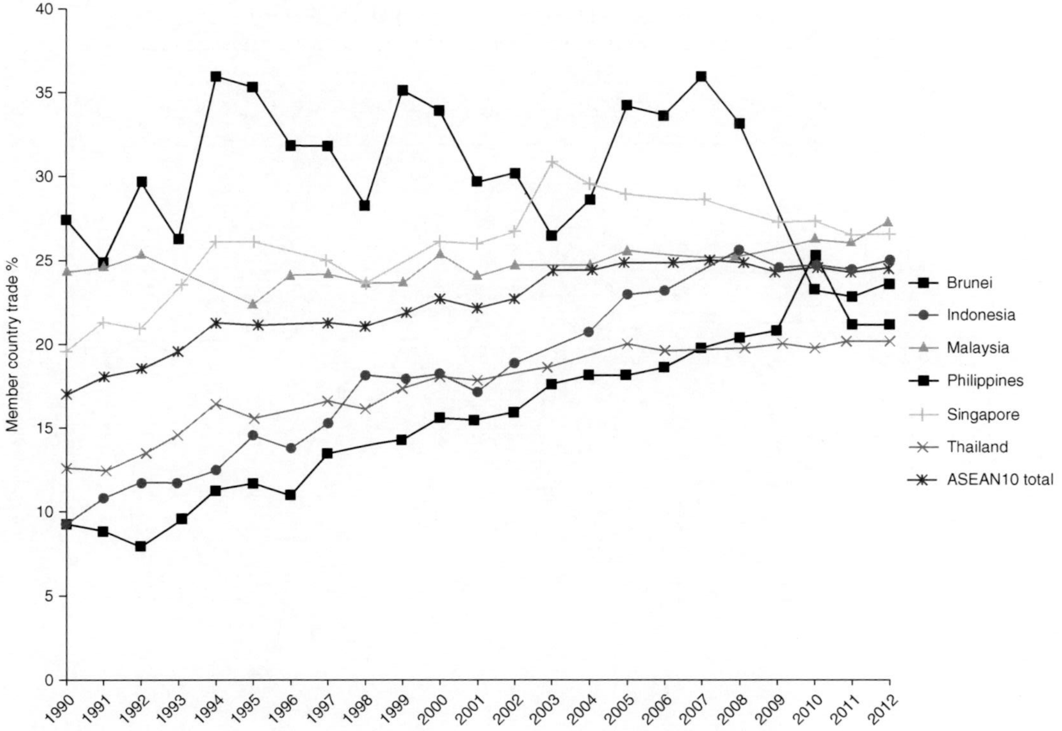

Figure 3.2a Intra-ASEAN share of member country total trade, 1990–2012 (Brunei, Indonesia, Malaysia, the Philippines, Singapore, Thailand)

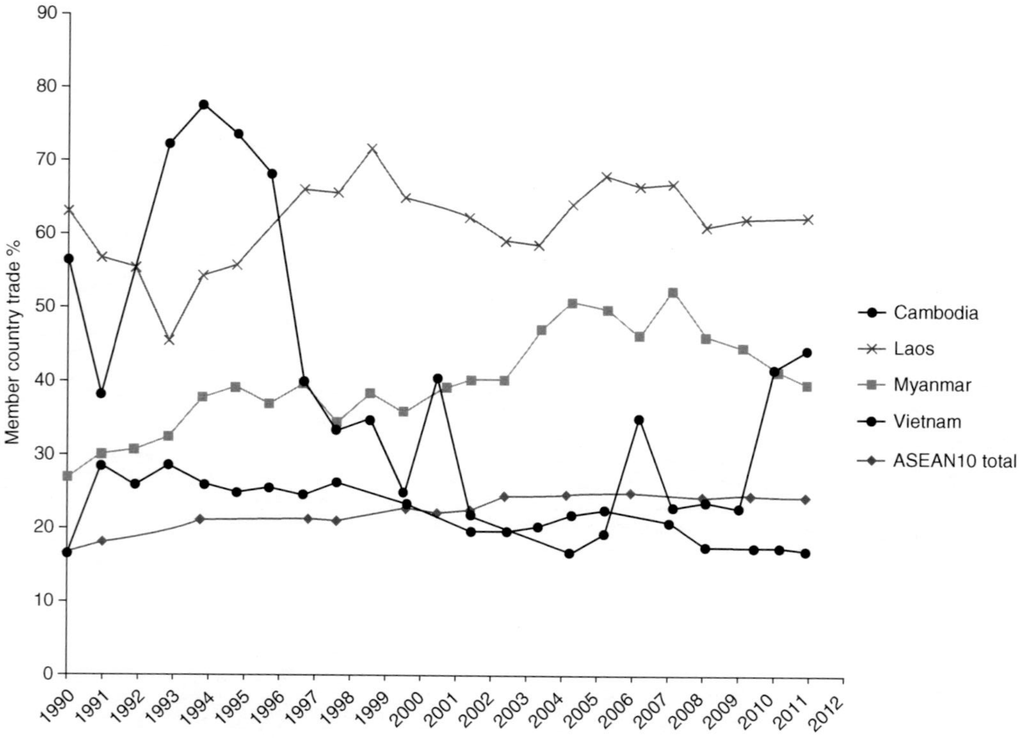

Figure 3.2b Intra-ASEAN share of member country total trade, 1990–2012 (Cambodia, Laos, Myanmar, Vietnam)
Source: IMF, Direction of Trade Statistics: www.elibrary.imf.org.

Brunei (though its importance has been declining since the beginning of the twin crises). Trends in the other economies are mixed. However, it is noteworthy that the ASEAN market share for each member economy tends to be above one-fifth for all economies save Vietnam, whose share has been about 18 per cent over the past few years (having fallen since Vietnam joined the World Trade Organization (WTO) and the normalisation of trade relations between Vietnam and the USA).

The most important points in considering the direction of ASEAN trade would, therefore, be: first, it is changing fairly rapidly, with China becoming increasingly important as ASEAN integrates into international and regional production networks and supply chains; second, intra-ASEAN trade is important to all ASEAN economies; and third, the majority of trade remains with non-ASEAN economies.

3.2 ASEAN's international trade in services

Services have been an increasingly important component of the ASEAN economies, and the potential for services trade has been progressively rising, owing in part to growth in such areas as information and communication technology (ICT) and finance. The ASEAN services sector contributes 40 per cent to 50 per cent of GDP on average, but for some economies these are dominated by non-tradable services.

Figures 3.3a and 3.3b summarise growth in services trade on an annual basis for the ASEAN6, CLMV and an ASEAN10 aggregate for the period 1980–2012. This growth

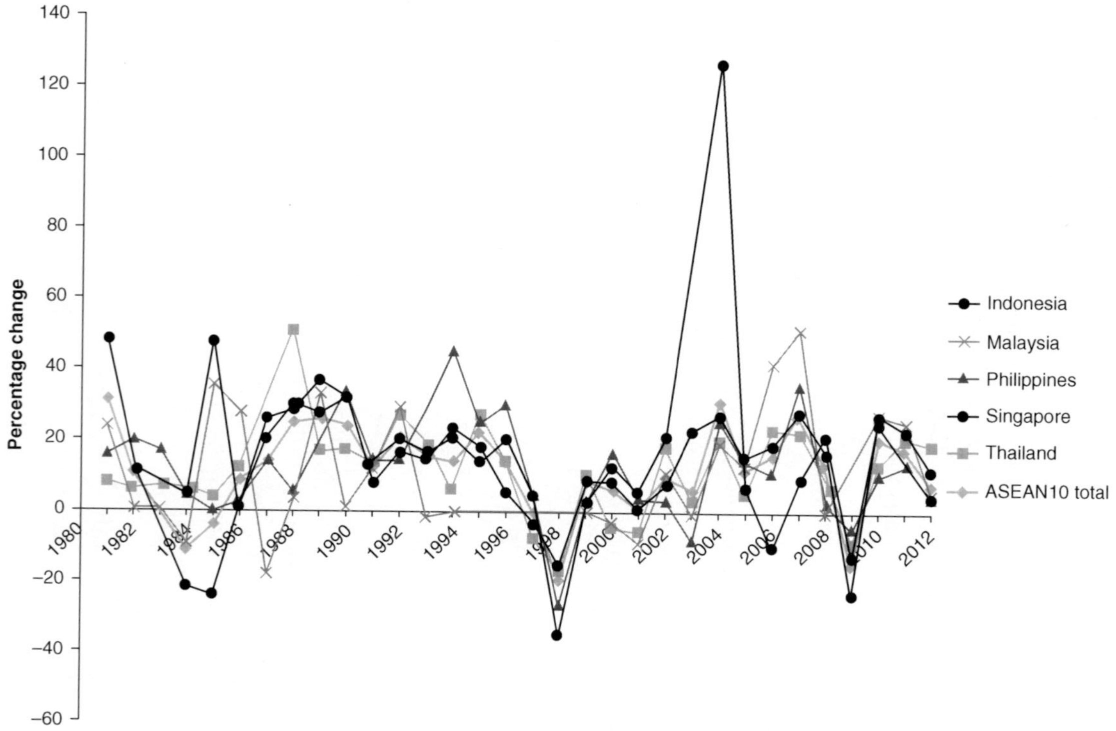

Figure 3.3a ASEAN services export growth, 1980–2012 (Indonesia, Malaysia, the Philippines, Singapore, Thailand)

Source: UNCTAD Handbook of Statistics.

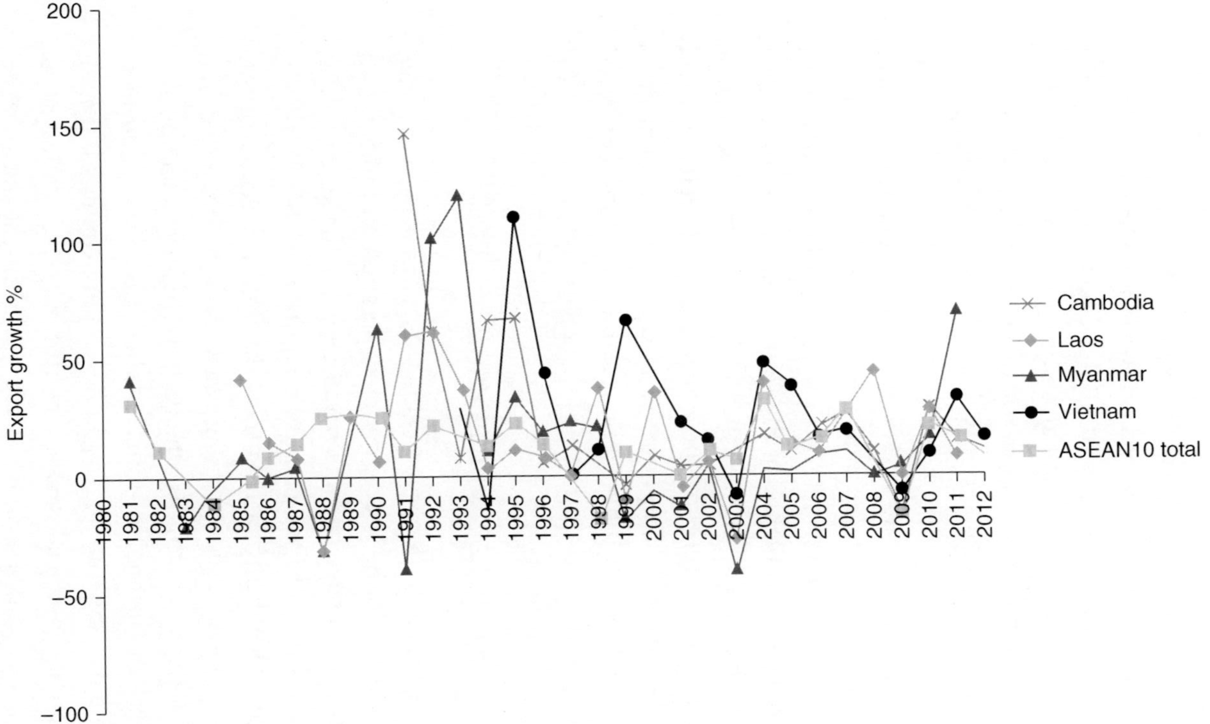

Figure 3.3b ASEAN services export growth, 1980–2012 (Cambodia, Laos, Myanmar, Vietnam)

Source: UNCTAD Handbook of Statistics.

has been impressive particularly in the ASEAN6 economies, though it is obviously cyclical, with large drops in growth rates during the AFC and at the beginning of the global financial crisis (GFC). What is not captured by the figures is the changing composition of services exports – financial and transportation services dominate Singapore's services exports while tourism services dominate in Cambodia. Statistically it is also very difficult to determine intra-ASEAN services trade, since balance of payments data do not usually report bilateral flows. Bilateral tourism data are more readily available: of the sources of visitors to ASEAN countries, those from other ASEAN countries formed nearly 50 per cent in the 2009–11 period, reflecting the neighbourhood effect boosted by improved transportation connectivity for tourist and business and student travel among ASEAN countries.

3.3 ASEAN's FDI inflows

Attracting FDI into the region has always been a major objective of ASEAN economic cooperation and integration. FDI inflows have become paramount for the success of an outward-oriented development strategy in the developing world. They bring in new (risk-sharing, non-debt-creating) capital flows, foreign exchange, easy access to foreign markets and foreign sourcing (particularly through production networks) and technology transfer. They also have a tendency to strengthen institutions within developing countries, including in the financial sector (see, for example, Prasad et al. 2006) and create a more stable environment and internal 'policy competition'.[2] In doing so, they establish an attractive business environment within which multinational corporations (MNCs) can profit from a vertical division of labour and production and facilitate the emergence of MNCs within the developing region itself. The diversity of economic structure and cost levels in the ASEAN region make it a particularly strong candidate for investment cooperation.

Table 3.1 summarises the performance of ASEAN economies in attracting FDI inflows over the 1995–2012 period. Several observations are worth noting. First, inward FDI flows have recovered since the AFC but have been volatile. In 2010, the year after the first USA-originated financial crisis, FDI reached almost US$98 billion, nearly doubling the 2008 value. By 2012, FDI grew to US$111 billion, a 14 per cent increase from 2010.

Second, Singapore is a big part of the ASEAN FDI story for most years, usually constituting more than 30 per cent of the ASEAN total (with 2008 being a notable exception) and reaching as high as 54 per cent of the ASEAN total in 2010. Third, since it joined the WTO, Vietnam has been one of the top FDI recipients in the region. Fourth, Indonesia has generally held the second largest share of the ASEAN total since recording negative inflows in 2000. While Vietnam held the second largest share in 2008, Indonesia more than doubled its FDI inflows from 2008 to 2012. Fifth, ASEAN has always

[2] By 'policy competition' we imply that countries within an FTA will have an incentive to adopt best practices, promote a low-cost business environment and embrace greater transparency if they are to compete effectively for FDI flows within a given trade area.

Table 3.1 *FDI inflows to ASEAN economies, China and India, selected years, 1995–2012*

	1995	2000	2005	2008	2010	2012
Brunei	582.76	549.61	289.48	330.06	625.67	850.00
Cambodia	150.70	148.50	381.18	815.18	782.60	1,557.14
Indonesia	4,419.00	−4,550.00	8,336.00	9,318.00	13,770.58	19,852.57
Laos	95.10	33.89	27.70	227.70	278.80	294.38
Malaysia	5,815.00	3,787.63	4,065.31	7,171.98	9,060.04	10,073.93
Myanmar	317.60	208.00	234.90	863.00	1,284.60	2,242.98
Philippines	1,459.00	2,240.00	1,854.00	1,544.00	1,298.00	2,797.00
Singapore	11,942.81	15,515.33	18,090.30	12,200.01	53,622.71	56,650.90
Thailand	2,070.00	3,410.12	8,066.55	8,454.70	9,146.78	8,607.45
Vietnam	1,780.40	1,298.00	1,954.00	9,579.00	8,000.00	8,368.00
ASEAN total	**28,632.37**	**22,641.08**	**43,299.43**	**50,503.62**	**97,869.77**	**111,294.34**
Other Asia						
China	37,520.53	40,714.81	72,406.00	108,312.00	114,734.00	121,080.00
India	2,151.00	3,587.99	7,621.77	47,138.73	21,125.45	25,542.84

Source: Compiled from UNCTAD and UNCTAD World Investment Report Annex Tables (for India and China).

pulled in significantly more FDI than India. On the other hand, FDI inflows into China have overtaken those into ASEAN since the AFC. However, this gap between China and ASEAN has narrowed in recent years. While China received two times the FDI flows of ASEAN in 2008, ASEAN's 2012 figures amounted to over 90 per cent of China's FDI inflows.

As shown in Table 3.2, intra-ASEAN FDI flows have been rising rapidly in the 2004–11 period, from 8.9 per cent of total FDI inflows in 2004 to 23 per cent of total FDI inflows in 2011, averaging 15.4 per cent over the period. The main ASEAN source countries are Singapore, with a 53 per cent share, followed by Malaysia, Indonesia and Thailand. The main ASEAN host countries are Singapore, with a 32 per cent share, followed by Indonesia (27 per cent), Thailand (15 per cent) and Malaysia (13 per cent). Singapore is a major investor in other ASEAN countries, but it also receives sizeable investments from Malaysia and Indonesia, particularly in services and real estate.

3.4 ASEAN commercial policy reforms

ASEAN's commercial policy has become increasingly open over time. But the majority of the region's economies still have a long path to tread in terms of commercial policy reform. Myriad economic studies on Asian growth and development stress that the ASEAN success story is based in large part on outward-oriented trade and investment.[3] Taking advantage of

[3] Asian Development Bank 2008 gives a survey of these studies.

Table 3.2 *FDI inflows into ASEAN from ASEAN countries, 2004–11 (US$ million)*

	2004	2005	2006	2007	2008	2009	2010	2011	2004–11
Source country									
Brunei	18.4	28.1	−37.4	−2.9	87.3	126.0	30.3	147.6	397.4
Indonesia	348.3	156.3	594.5	241.3	867.1	968.8	1,458.9	1,361.0	5,996.0
Malaysia	1,187.0	1,355.1	897.3	980.4	3,422.6	2,632.0	2,859.8	2,485.9	15,820.1
Philippines	153.6	69.4	156.6	334.6	−221.1	−410.3	245.4	127.4	455.5
Singapore	1,593.3	2,567.5	6,663.7	6,421.1	4,611.2	2,218.2	7,990.5	11,579.9	43,645.5
Thailand	196.3	10.2	269.1	884.9	816.9	590.9	1,203.9	679.2	4,653.5
Cambodia	3.4	0.0	0.0	1.3	13.1	-6.0	37.7	56.8	106.4
Laos	0.0	−0.2	41.6	9.7	−72.1	0.4	34.5	0.6	14.5
Myanmar	7.2	14.7	49.7	62.9	64.5	71.1	68.9	141.2	480.3
Vietnam	7.1	9.4	6.7	179.7	139.3	109.3	392.9	294.4	1138.9
ASEAN10	3,516.6	4,210.6	8,641.9	9,113.0	9,728.9	6,300.2	14,322.7	26,270.7	82,104.6
Host country									
Brunei	19.1	19.6	9.8	62.1	0.9	3.1	89.5	67.5	271.5
Indonesia	204.2	883.3	1,353.9	1,108.2	3,398.0	1,380.1	5,904.4	8,338.2	22,570.3
Malaysia	980.2	720.9	461.6	3,780.1	1,645.5	−60.2	525.6	2,664.3	10,718.0
Philippines	71.1	3.4	705.4	−705.1	307.8	−4.9	40.2	−107.0	311.0
Singapore	1,261.5	1,143.1	1,065.6	1,366.8	771.2	2,791.1	4,569.0	13,213.4	26,181.7
Thailand	688.7	1,101.3	4,626.5	2,489.4	508.4	1,463.2	1,236.9	317.1	12,431.6

Cambodia	31.9	129.2	155.5	271.2	240.9	174.0	349.0	223.8	1,575.6
Laos	7.8	6.7	10.6	100.4	47.7	57.3	135.4	54.0	419.8
Myanmar	9.3	38.4	71.0	93.5	103.5	67.8	171.7	na	555.1
Vietnam	242.9	164.7	182.0	546.3	2,705.0	428.7	1,300.9	1,499.4	7,069.9
ASEAN10	3,516.6	4,210.6	6,641.9	9,113.0	9,728.9	6,300.2	14,322.7	26,270.7	82,104.6
Inflows from world	39,386.4	42,556.4	63,689.2	84,152.4	49,289.7	46,896.7	92,278.6	114,110.6	532,360.2
ASEAN percentage of world	8.9	9.9	10.4	10.8	19.7	13.4	15.5	23.0	15.4

Source: ASEAN Statistical Yearbook 2012.

international markets requires that many variables be in place, including macroeconomic stability, correct microeconomic signals, necessary infrastructure, forward-looking government policy (for example, in terms of developing human capital, capacity building, information dissemination regarding international markets and overcoming market failures) and a well-prepared private sector, including for FDI. These conditions cannot be created overnight; they often take a great deal of time, trial and error and patience before outward-orientation can bear fruit.

Commercial policy reforms in ASEAN countries over the years are reflected in the following.

3.4.1 Tariffs

One way to capture the reform process is an analysis of applied most-favoured nation (MFN) tariff levels at the WTO, as shown in Table 3.3 at the HS 1-digit level for the latest year for which data are available, and in Table 3.4 for 2001 in order to show changes over the past decade. Corresponding tariff levels for China and India are included for comparative purposes. Several observations are worth noting.

- First, Singapore is essentially a free-trade economy and has been so for a long time.[4] Brunei has cut tariffs essentially to

[4] It should be noted that while Singapore's applied MFN tariffs are zero (except for six items of alcoholic beverage), its bound MFN tariffs are positive. The gap between bound and applied tariffs is the policy space Singapore has to raise MFN tariffs legitimately (without attracting retaliation by WTO trading partners) in the future if so required by economic circumstances.

Table 3.3 *Average tariffs (applied MFN) at the HS 1-digit level, latest year*

Product	Product name	Brunei (2010)	Cambodia (2008)	Indonesia (2010)	Laos (2008)	Malaysia (2009)	Myanmar (2008)	Philippines (2010)	Singapore (2010)	Thailand (2009)	Vietnam (2010)	CHN (2010)	IND (2009)
0	Animal and animal products; vegetable products	0.00	16.02	5.22	21.52	2.86	8.31	11.19	0.00	22.09	14.49	12.68	36.89
1	Foodstuffs	0.00	14.83	4.65	12.55	2.77	5.65	10.86	0.00	21.03	16.45	15.55	24.70
2	Mineral products; chemicals and allied industries	0.02	13.92	5.72	9.72	1.37	5.10	3.82	0.00	7.57	9.41	7.00	14.70
3	Plastics/rubber	0.88	10.98	6.71	9.85	7.47	4.20	6.01	0.00	6.37	7.22	8.10	9.82
4	Raw hides, skins, leather, furs; wood and wood products	4.70	13.40	5.10	13.33	3.96	6.74	5.95	0.00	7.83	11.67	7.37	9.34
5	Textiles	0.66	10.48	8.57	8.47	9.85	8.09	8.16	0.00	5.57	8.40	9.07	10.02
6	Footwear, headgear; stone	1.09	20.30	12.85	10.11	16.25	13.11	12.38	0.00	23.50	18.81	14.87	9.79
7	Glass; Metals	0.44	11.33	7.38	5.30	19.78	3.45	5.88	0.00	5.91	8.16	7.83	7.13
8	Metals; machinery/ electrical; transportation	8.39	17.63	7.32	11.94	8.79	5.41	6.68	0.00	9.51	10.40	8.83	10.38
9	Miscellaneous manufactured goods	5.78	16.52	7.02	10.32	5.18	6.51	4.87	0.00	9.67	10.13	10.23	8.89

Source: Compiled from UN TRAINS, via World Bank WITS database.

Table 3.4 *Average tariffs (applied MFN) at the HS 1-digit level, 2001*

Product	Product name	Brunei	Cambodia	Indonesia	Laos	Malaysia	Myanmar	Philippines	Singapore	Thailand	Vietnam	CHN	IND
0	Animal and animal products; vegetable products	0.00	17.49	5.06	23.49	4.25	9.18	16.19	0.00	29.31	24.48	18.60	36.95
1	Foodstuffs	0.00	17.98	4.65	12.32	4.45	5.54	13.08	0.00	23.37	18.61	28.19	43.43
2	Mineral products; chemicals and allied industries	0.02	14.93	8.29	7.70	3.08	3.26	4.35	0.00	8.08	10.13	10.63	34.21
3	Plastics/rubber	1.08	12.89	6.82	8.90	8.77	3.95	5.46	0.00	17.70	9.53	13.60	33.42
4	Raw hides, skins, leather, furs; wood and wood products	3.57	19.39	4.00	12.49	3.68	5.59	7.12	0.00	16.40	14.61	13.76	28.49
5	Textiles	0.33	13.50	8.22	8.22	15.14	7.47	8.25	0.00	17.02	26.71	19.24	28.54
6	Footwear, headgear; stone	1.18	26.39	12.17	9.92	19.60	12.25	16.11	0.00	31.07	41.86	22.82	34.77
7	Glass; Metals	0.54	14.45	8.08	5.37	11.62	4.17	6.45	0.00	14.61	10.24	10.71	33.46
8	Metals; machinery/ electrical; transportation	9.66	18.34	6.26	7.77	20.13	3.25	4.95	0.00	17.31	12.07	15.56	28.99
9	Miscellaneous manufactured goods	5.53	17.61	7.49	10.11	7.82	6.43	5.62	0.00	11.67	14.59	16.19	30.17

Source: Compiled from UN TRAINS, via World Bank WITS database.

zero for most sectors except machinery and transport equipment and miscellaneous manufactures.

- Second, in Indonesia, Malaysia, the Philippines and Thailand, tariffs on manufactures have generally come down, and sometimes significantly, with average tariffs being less than 10 per cent in all sectors except footwear, which nonetheless experienced significant decreases in tariffs since 2001 in all countries. The only manufactured good with tariffs above 10 per cent in which tariffs actually increased was glass and metals in Malaysia, which rose from 13 per cent to 20 per cent.
- Third, Vietnam's tariffs have come down in all commodity categories, and in some cases impressively so. This reflects the liberalisation process that it adopted as it applied successfully for accession to the WTO.
- Fourth, in comparing ASEAN average tariffs to China and India, we find that, besides Cambodia, Myanmar and Laos, tariff levels are usually lower in ASEAN, particularly outside of manufactures.

3.4.2 *Non-tariff barriers*

Data on non-tariff barriers (NTBs) are notoriously difficult to obtain.[5] Not all non-tariff measures (NTMs) may be considered as barriers to international trade. However, their evaluation is fraught with difficulties, since they vary greatly in terms of substance. We may know exactly what the

[5] This review draws from Plummer and Chia 2009: ch. 1.

(static) economic effects of an import quota would be, for example, by calculating a tariff equivalent but not a required licensing arrangement. The effects of the latter would certainly be less restrictive if the licensing arrangement were more or less automatic as opposed to discretionary, but how does one distinguish this difference in the data on the presence of this type of NTB? Moreover, should anti-dumping duties be included in the list of NTBs? Most economists would agree that anti-dumping duties tend to be protectionist in nature rather than compensating for some nefarious pricing strategy of foreign firms. But one cannot deny that dumping sometimes occurs, and anti-dumping duties are permitted by the WTO (under certain general guidelines). In any event, classifying anti-dumping in some aggregate measure of NTBs might be theoretically correct but extremely complicated.

The Uruguay Round made substantial progress in addressing NTBs, particularly in the area of 'tarifficating' existing quotas in many sensitive agricultural products and doing away with 'orderly marketing arrangements' such as the Multi-Fibre Arrangement (MFA), which was phased out under the Uruguay Round Agreement on Textiles and Clothing. In fact, some of the changes in tariffs – particularly in agriculture – were less impressive or even rose owing to this process of transforming NTBs into more transparent and less problematic tariffs, which were then normalised and rendered easier to liberalise. There are still complicated arrangements in agriculture but things have been greatly improved with the Uruguay Round, and quotas are supposed to be a thing of the past.

Feridhanusetyawan (2005) has generated trade restrictiveness indices for Asia, including NTBs. This gives us a general indication of the degree of importance of NTBs in the region's economies. The restrictiveness of NTBs is categorised into three groups: restrictive, intermediate and open. The only economy receiving a clean bill of health for NTBs in ASEAN would be Singapore. The other ASEAN6 economies fall in the intermediate range, and Vietnam (which joined the WTO after the numbers were compiled), Laos and Myanmar fall in the restrictive range.

In sum, NTBs notwithstanding, there has been extensive reform of commercial policies in the ASEAN region almost without exception. Rather than retreating into protectionism and raising trade barriers as defensive measures in the wake of the AFC, the Crisis-affected economies bravely and correctly took the exact opposite path and liberalised further. ASEAN's transitional economies had also to put in completely new commercial-policy regimes as part of the process. Notwithstanding these developments, there still exist high tariffs in certain sectors and, even within sectors with seemingly low averages, tariff spikes. NTBs continue to be a problem in many countries, though there is evidence of considerable improvement. In other words, commercial policy liberalisation has been impressive but much more needs to be done.

3.5 ASEAN production networks and market-driven integration

Production networks (international and regional) are market-driven and refer to the breaking up of production processes into fragmented segments that can be carried out in different cross-border locations and eventually coordinated for assembly into final products. This process and development has been further facilitated by FTAs that encourage inward FDI by MNCs through trade and investment liberalisation and regulatory reforms and harmonisation. These investments are usually found in industries with long value chains, such as electronics and electrical machinery, automotives and textiles and garments.

As ASEAN countries embarked on outward-oriented development strategies and undertook unilateral and FTA-led trade and investment liberalisation, intra-ASEAN and extra-ASEAN trade and investment have been on a rising trend. Production networks have played a significant role by relocating labour-intensive segments to low wage economies, resulting in rapidly growing intra-industry trade in parts and components. Production networks make use of each economy's advantages to boost productivity and cut costs, while bolstering investment and technological transfer.

Athukorala (2010) identified the following factors in the rapid growth of production networks in Northeast Asia and ASEAN. First, the region has wide differences in wage and labour productivity levels, thus enabling a wide choice of competitive cost locations for different parts of the value chain. Second, trade and investment liberalisation and facilitation, as well as availability of efficient infrastructure and strong intra-regional and international links, result in lower production and logistics costs. Third, the first wave of successful investments to core ASEAN countries led to the spread of production network investments to other ASEAN economies.

Figure 3.4 shows the trend growth in parts and components exports of ASEAN countries. Countries with a constant growth in shares are Singapore and Malaysia. Thailand has experienced a declining trend in share since the AFC, indicating its new importance as an assembly base.

More than 90 per cent of Northeast Asia and ASEAN's exports are now manufactures of growing sophistication and dominated by electronics. More than 70 per cent of intra-East Asian trade comprises trade in parts and components that are further produced and re-exported to the rest of the world, particularly developed country markets in the USA and EU.[6] Over 60 per cent of total Asian exports is eventually destined for outside the region, particularly the USA and EU. This highlights the vulnerability of ASEAN and other East Asian exports to external shocks such as the ongoing US and EU crises, as demonstrated by the slowdown in manufactures and parts and components exports of most ASEAN countries in 2012.

The regional division of manufacturing production and export appears as follows: China, Japan and South Korea are the home countries for production networks in machinery and parts; the regional hub of these production networks is increasingly China, which functions as the major assembly base; Singapore, Thailand, Malaysia and the Philippines are growing exporters of machinery parts and components (with some of the highest parts and components trade to GDP in the

[6] See Asian Development Bank 2008 for detailed discussions.

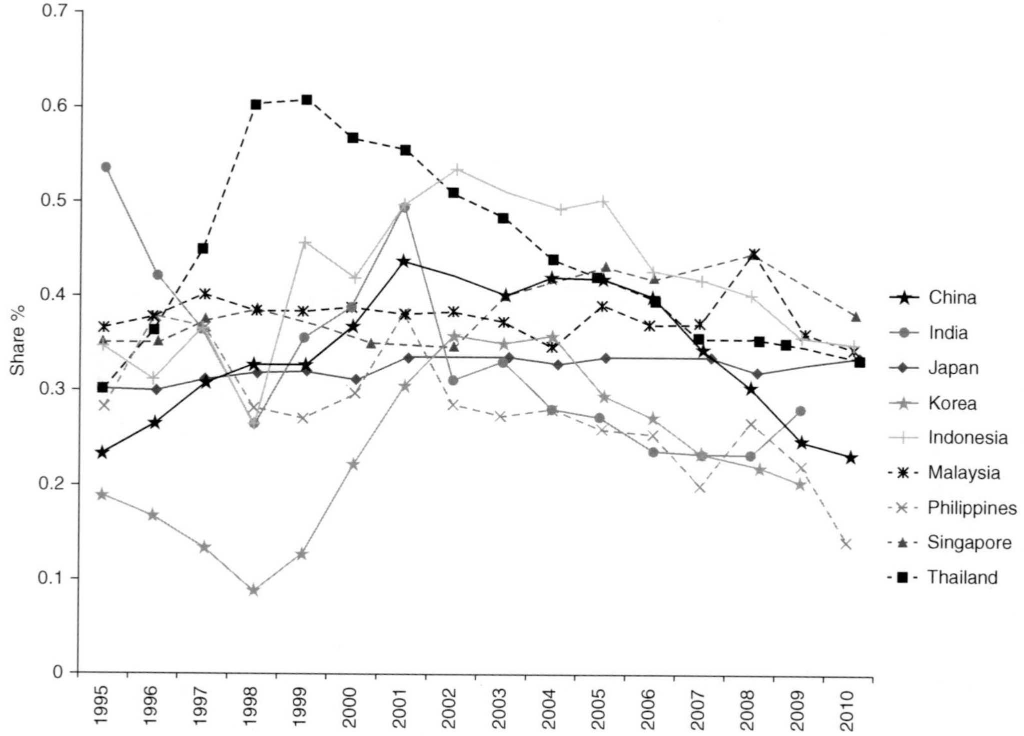

Figure 3.4 Share of parts and components exports in total machinery and parts exports from selected countries to ASEAN, 1995–2010

Source: S. Chayodom and K. Cheewatratoolpong, 'The Impact of the AEC on ASEAN Production Networks', background for the ASEAN 2030 study, Asian Development Bank Institute mimeo (2012); calculated from the UN Comtrade Statistics.

world). Success of these first-wave ASEAN countries, based on policies that encourage inflows of MNC investments, effective transfer and absorption of new production technologies, growth of local supporting industries and local suppliers and globalised links, has enabled the spread of production networks to other neighbouring ASEAN economies. This enables the less-developed ASEAN economies to specialise in narrower niches, and enter international markets requiring only a more limited range of skills.

What role does ASEAN play in the rapidly expanding trade by production networks? Although production networks are essentially market-driven, trade and investment liberalisation and facilitation under AFTA, AFAS, AIA and AEC as well as industrial complementation under ASEAN Industrial Cooperation (AICO) have encouraged FDI by MNCs and the location of multi-plants in the ASEAN region, the most apparent being in the electronics and automotive sectors. While studies have shown that utilisation of AFTA tariff preferences has been low,[7] improvements in ASEAN customs and standards harmonisation have facilitated trade flows, while investment liberalisation, facilitation and protection have attracted MNCs to establish operations in different ASEAN locations. More particularly, participation in ASEAN trade and investment liberalisation and facilitation programmes have also resulted in production networks spreading from the core ASEAN countries to the less-developed CLMV countries.

[7] See, for example, Kawai and Wignaraja 2011.

ASEAN needs to build upon its existing production networks. ASEAN collectively and individually must move up the global value chain and strive to become innovators. The more advanced countries such as Singapore, Malaysia and Thailand will need to deepen their competitive advantage in existing production networks and clusters (for example, biotechnology in Singapore, electronics in Malaysia and the automotive sector in Thailand). With dynamic changes in competitive advantages, some of their industrial segments need to relocate to other ASEAN countries with lower wage costs, such as Indonesia, the Philippines and CLMV. For the first-wave countries, new industrial clusters will emerge.

Chapter 4

ASEAN's FTA-led economic integration

4.1 ASEAN economic cooperation in the pre-AFTA period, 1977–91

Prior to the late 1980s, consideration of deep regional economic integration remained taboo and the focus was on economic cooperation.[1] This period was characterised by preoccupation with commodity trade problems, the ASEAN Preferential Trading Arrangement (PTA) and industrial cooperation schemes. Akrasanee (2000: 36–7) notes:

> [T]o counter the growing influence of communist/socialist states the member countries decided to strengthen ASEAN as the defining regional community. Economic cooperation was adopted as a means to serve the purpose . . . The PTA was intended for ASEAN markets to become more accessible to the member countries and more integrated. For large-scale capital intensive projects, joint investments with proper division of responsibilities would benefit from economies of scale.[2]

[1] In the context of ASEAN, deep economic cooperation refers to policy measures to facilitate trade and industrial development by removing subjective and objective frictions and obstacles. Economic integration refers to the objective of forming an FTA, customs union or economic community.

[2] Akrasanee 2000.

4.1.1 Initial obstacles and subsequent rationale

ASEAN's preference for regional economic cooperation rather than deep integration in the 1970s and 1980s reflects the reluctance of some ASEAN countries to undertake trade and investment liberalisation owing to the pursuit of industrial policies of import substitution and picking winners.[3] However, as the limitations of import substitution became increasingly apparent,[4] more countries favoured an export-oriented development strategy with greater acceptance of trade and investment liberalisation unilaterally and under ASEAN.

Another obstacle to deep economic integration in ASEAN at the time was the diversity in size, resource endowment, level of economic development, technological capability and openness of trade and investment regimes among ASEAN countries that led to differing perceptions of benefits and costs of economic integration. It was perceived that the more competitive ASEAN economies would gain more. There is also the political economy dimension of trade and investment liberalisation within each country. The winners include consumers (the silent majority) who

[3] Severino 2006 reported the views of the then Indonesian economic minister Widjojo: Indonesia resisted all notions of trade liberalisation and regional economic integration and was more concerned with food as well as energy security and with the establishment of large-scale industrial projects.

[4] There were a number of academic studies that showed the limitations and high costs of industrialisation based on import substitution strategies pursued in the developing world, particularly in Latin America. See, for example, Little et al. 1970; also Baer 1972.

enjoy lower prices and wider range of goods and services; farmers, businesses and workers in expanding export sectors; and foreign investors able to have right of establishment and a level playing field. The vocal opposition includes uncompetitive farmers and businesses and workers in sectors threatened by import competition. National policy makers thus have the difficult task of persuading (and compensating) the losers to accept change and helping them to relocate from uncompetitive to competitive sectors.

The first ASEAN Economic Ministers' Meeting (AEMM) took place only in March 1976 even though ASEAN was formed in 1967. There was preoccupation with commodities trade (since that was the structure of ASEAN exports then). For some countries there was also concern over access to critical supplies of rice and crude oil and ASEAN agreed to cooperate by giving each other priority access to food and energy in 'critical circumstances' such as natural disasters. Also agreed were a preferential trading arrangement and the establishment of large-scale industrial projects that would use available materials, increase food production, save foreign exchange and create jobs.

4.1.2 ASEAN Preferential Trading Arrangement

In July 1977 ASEAN ratified the ASEAN Preferential Trading Arrangement (PTA)[5] under which each ASEAN country

[5] In the typology of economic integration, the lowest level is represented by partial preferential trading arrangement, followed by FTA, customs union, common market and economic community.

would grant to imports from other member states a margin of preference on MFN tariffs. The PTA would cover 'basic commodities', particularly food and energy, products of the industrial cooperation schemes and lists of goods to be negotiated among the parties. The PTA scheme was based on product-by-product negotiation, initially covering seventy-one product items and reaching 15,295 by 1990, but the actual volume of trade covered did not grow correspondingly. The initial margin of preference of 10 per cent was increased to 20 per cent to 25 per cent in 1980 and the initial cut-off import value of US$50,000 was eventually abolished in 1984. In 1987 the economic ministers signed a protocol committing ASEAN countries to place in the PTA within five years (for Indonesia and the Philippines seven years) at least 90 per cent of items traded among them with at least 50 per cent of the value of intra-ASEAN trade; the margin of preference for the new items was raised to 25 per cent and for those already in the PTA to 50 per cent; the ASEAN content requirement was to be reduced in five years from 50 per cent to 35 per cent (42 per cent for Indonesia) and on a case-by-case basis after five years, but could be brought back up to the 50 per cent level.

The ASEAN PTA was generally considered a failure, with considerable negotiating resources expanded producing only a limited impact on intra-ASEAN trade. The 1991 AEMM concluded that while intra-ASEAN trade in items covered by the PTA had grown from US$121 million in 1987 to US$578 million in 1989, it still accounted for an insignificant proportion of total intra-ASEAN trade.[6] What were the reasons for

[6] See Severino 2006: 216.

the PTA's failure? With tariff liberalisation based on time-consuming product-by-product negotiations rather than across-the-board and the prevalent import substituting industrialisation policies, the lack of seriousness to liberalise intra-ASEAN trade was highlighted by inclusion of snow ploughs and nuclear plants in the negotiations and the long national exclusion lists.

Additionally, a 1986 UNIDO study highlighted underlying structural difficulties and institutional biases.[7] First, existing trade and production patterns had allowed only limited absorptive capacity in the ASEAN countries for each other's major exports such as rubber, tin, timber, palm oil and coconut products that are primarily destined for demand outside the region, except for Thai export of rice. Second, the ASEAN economies at that stage of economic development had almost exhausted their commercial capacities in responding to the large and growing export markets of developed countries. Third, import-substituting industrialisation policies and balance of payments difficulties faced by some ASEAN countries had resulted in certain policies that were inherently biased against regional trade, that is, high priority for the import of capital and intermediate goods that are usually sourced from developed countries.

4.1.3 ASEAN industrial cooperation

In the 1970s and 1980s ASEAN also dabbled in a number of industrial cooperation schemes, namely, the 1976 ASEAN

[7] United Nations Industrial Development Organization 1986.

Industrial Projects (AIPs), 1981 ASEAN Industrial Complementation (AIC) and 1983 ASEAN Industrial Joint Ventures (AIJVs).[8] The AIP programme had a chequered history, reflecting inadequate studies on project feasibility, a top-down approach and conflicts between national industrial policies and attempts at regional industrial cooperation. Five AIPs were allocated, with urea fertiliser plant each for Indonesia and Malaysia, superphosphates for the Philippines, diesel engines for Singapore and soda ash for Thailand. Each of the five projects was estimated to require an investment of US$250–300 million. In 1977 Japanese Prime Minister Fukuda offered to extend financing in the form of soft loans up to a total of US$1 billion for the AIPs, provided feasibility studies bore out their viability. In March 1980 ASEAN governments signed the Basic Agreement on ASEAN Industrial Projects formulating the conditions for the five projects agreed earlier and other projects to be allocated in the future – the host country would invest 60 per cent of equity, with the other four ASEAN members taking the remaining 40 per cent in equal shares. The agreement had provisions on taxation, incentives, repatriation of capital and remittance of profits, protection of minority shareholders, pricing and bankruptcy.

Of the five approved AIPs, only the urea fertiliser plants in Aceh (Indonesia) and Bintulu (Malaysia) survived as such. For the Philippines there were a number of changes to its allocated project – in 1979 it substituted the

[8] See Severino 2006: 213–22 (ch. 5).

superphosphate project with one that would produce ammonium sulphate fertiliser, changed again to a proposal for a pulp and paper plant, and changed again to a copper fabrication plant that the ASEAN economic ministers eventually approved in 1982. Likewise, there were changes to Thailand's allocated soda ash project as, facing technical difficulties, it decided to replace it with potash mining that ASEAN economic ministers finally approved in 1990. However, Thailand had to take up 71 per cent of the equity as Indonesia and Malaysia agreed to commit only 13 per cent each while Brunei, the Philippines and Singapore agreed to commit a token 1 per cent each. The Thai government eventually decided to pull out of the project and turned it over to the private sector. For Singapore, its allocated diesel engines project also met with difficulties as its ASEAN partners refused to open their markets for diesel engines below 200 horsepower, which accounted for the bulk of the ASEAN market. Singapore gave up the diesel engine project in favour of hepatitis-B vaccines but other ASEAN countries contributed only a token 1 per cent each of the equity. Singapore eventually withdrew the hepatitis-B project as an AIP.

The AIC was formalised in 1981 and provided for allocation of 'complementary' industrial products for manufacture by at least four ASEAN countries (or fewer, if approved by ASEAN economic ministers). Before that, in 1980 the ASEAN economic ministers had already adopted two complementation packages involving automotive parts. Products of AIC packages were to enjoy exclusive privileges: no AIC participant could manufacture the same product already allocated to another participant, with two years of exclusivity for existing products and three years for new products. Additionally, AIC products would qualify for preferences under the PTA with a 50 per cent tariff margin of preference.

In 1988 ASEAN augmented the AIC programme with brand-to-brand (B-to-B) complementation specifically for the automotive industry to enhance vertical FDI across ASEAN member states. It provided a 50 per cent tariff margin of preference for specified parts and components of vehicles of a particular brand traded among approved ASEAN participants. Interested countries would negotiate individual packages for ASEAN approval. Malaysia, the Philippines and Thailand were the initial participants, joined later by Indonesia. The first B-to-B complementation schemes were approved in 1989 with proposals from Mitsubishi, Volvo and Mercedes-Benz, followed in 1990 by proposals from Toyota, Nissan, DAF (Belgium), Mitsubishi and Volvo. In 1991 the B-to-B complementation scheme was expanded to cover non-automotive items as well, but by then the industrial complementation schemes were about to be superseded by the ASEAN Free Trade Area (AFTA) and the ASEAN Industrial Cooperation (AICO) programmes.

Under the 1983 AIJV programme, projects needed equity participation of at least two ASEAN countries to enjoy a 50 per cent tariff margin of preference from the participating countries for the first four years and market exclusivity for three years, provided they were 'new' products, after which non-participating ASEAN member states had to extend the same margin of preference. In December 1987 a revised AIJV agreement enlarged the margin of preference to 90 per cent and more-attractive equity schemes introduced also produced disappointing results owing to bureaucratic costs and confusions in regional and national legal applications. By 1989, six years after launching the AIJV programme, the ASEAN economic ministers noted the 'slow progress' in the approval of AIJV projects. By 1991 enamel, heavy equipment, aluminium hydroxide and Nestlé projects had been approved.[9]

In summary, the various industrial cooperation schemes failed because ASEAN countries were engaged in industrial policies of import substitution and building national champions resulting in conflicting national interests. The schemes highlighted national differences and did not contribute significantly to industrial development of ASEAN countries (except for B-to-B complementation in the automotive sector and Nestlé's multi-country plants).

[9] Nestlé (a Swiss conglomerate) demonstrated the success of the AIJV. It put up a production plant with regional capacities in Indonesia, Malaysia, Singapore, Thailand and the Philippines. The idea was for each of them to become a production centre for a particular product to be distributed within ASEAN and other Asian countries. Brunei was an equity participant in the project. Indonesia was to produce soya-based beverages; Malaysia, bouillon, chocolate wafers and chocolate dragées; Singapore, soya-source powder; Thailand, non-dairy creamer; and the Philippines, breakfast cereals. The products were selected so that the benefits would accrue not only to ASEAN as a whole but to each member country. The location of each of the plants was determined according to demand patterns based on market knowledge. After almost ten years, the Nestlé AIJV successfully achieved various objectives (see Severino 2006: 229).

4.2 ASEAN economic integration in the AFTA period, 1992–2002

4.2.1 The rationale

From the late 1980s dramatic global and regional developments were pressuring ASEAN to move towards regional economic integration so as to compete effectively for global markets and investments. The Uruguay Round was completed in December 1991 and GATT was being reorganised into the WTO; the EU was being created by the Treaty of Maastricht in February 1992; the North American Free Trade Area (NAFTA) was being negotiated and finally signed in December 1992; radical economic reforms were taking place in China and followed by India, laying the foundation for their accelerated economic growth in the coming decade.

Proposals from a number of ASEAN member states on economic integration were put up, including an improved PTA, a Common Effective Preferential Tariff (CEPT) scheme, and AFTA.[10] The AEMM in October 1991 considered them and declared in their joint statement:

> The Ministers, in acknowledging the interrelationship of the new initiatives, agreed that all member countries

[10] It is to be noted that the Agreement on the Common Effective Preferential Tariff Scheme for the ASEAN Free Trade Area contained only six pages, in contrast to the almost 400 pages of the NAFTA agreement. The latter was also preceded by lengthy and exhaustive studies, while the CEPT did not undergo a similar process.

> should subscribe to the establishment of AFTA simultaneously so as to create within the time frame of 15 years a truly liberalised ASEAN market with the CEPT in the range of 0–5% for manufactured products. They also agreed that AFTA shall be effected mainly through the CEPT scheme, while the improved Preferential Trading Arrangements (PTA) scheme will continue to be applied as a complementary tool. . . . The Ministers agreed that the establishment of AFTA with the application of CEPT on a sectoral basis within the definite time frame would serve the interest of all member countries, accommodate the respective national conditions and requirements, lead to the emergence of the ASEAN region as a truly liberalised market, and maintain ASEAN's relevance in the world at large beyond the 1990s.
>
> Severino 2006: 223–4

It is to be noted that Thailand's proposal for an AFTA had listed four arguments:

- Subjecting ASEAN countries' industries to regional competition would help prepare them for the more liberal global trading regime following the conclusion of the Uruguay Round.
- Freeing trade within ASEAN would attract MNC investments setting up multi-plant operations in line with globalisation of industrial production and increase ASEAN's industrial exports.
- The emerging European Single Market and NAFTA required ASEAN countries to coalesce economically in order to avoid becoming very insignificant in international economic negotiations.

- ASEAN would be participating in APEC and the proposed East Asia Economic Group more effectively if it were to do so 'as a strong economic entity'.[11]

The fourth ASEAN Summit in Singapore in 1992 approved the AFTA initiative. Severino (2006) reported the rationale given by its two strongest advocates, namely, Thai Prime Minister Anand Panyarachun and Singapore Prime Minister Goh Chok Tong.

Anand Panyarachun:

> In the short run AFTA could result in initial losses of government revenue. Inefficient sectors would become vulnerable to competition. Industrial restructuring and readjustment could also lead to temporary unemployment in some countries . . . Nevertheless the overall long term benefits of AFTA will more than compensate for any short-term loss. . . . Besides freer flow of trade, AFTA would lead to a larger ASEAN market of 360 million that would be more attractive for investments both from within and without than 6 separate markets. With economies of scale, this would also lead to a rational allocation of resources and increased efficiency in production. ASEAN would be in much better position to attract investment as goods would be produced more economically and sold at a more competitive price.
>
> Severino 2006: 224

Goh Chok Tong:

> The flow of private investments is decided by hard-headed businessmen on the basis of expected returns on

[11] See Severino 2006: 223.

> capital. They will locate their companies where they assess the companies to enjoy the greatest competitive advantage, that is, where they can manufacture their products at the lowest cost, enjoy the largest domestic markets, and face the least uncertainty. . . . Unless ASEAN can match the other regions in attractiveness both as a base for investments as well as a market for their products, investments by MNCs are likely to flow away from our part of the world to the Single European Market and NAFTA. If we do not synergise our strengths, ASEAN will risk missing the boat.
>
> Severino 2006: 224

The case for economic integration was pushed top-down as, unlike in countries such as the USA and Japan, the ASEAN private sector was notably silent in lobbying for economic integration. Local businesses appeared not to be ready for external competition or were not ready to export or venture abroad and so did not see economic integration as directly benefiting them. This is borne out by the fact that the corporate participants of the B-to-B industrial complementation were primarily foreign MNCs, and local small and medium-sized enterprises (SMEs) were slow to utilise the AFTA tariff preferences.[12]

ASEAN agreed to establish the AFTA in January 1992, with intra-ASEAN tariff liberalisation and elimination under the CEPT scheme. A customs union with common external tariffs was ruled out in view of the marked differences in

[12] See Kawai and Wignaraja 2011.

MFN tariff levels among ASEAN economies, particularly between Singapore and the other ASEAN member states. By the early 1990s economic integration elsewhere in the world, for example, NAFTA, had moved beyond traditional free trade in goods to encompass services and investments. Hence AFTA was complemented by the 1995 AFAS and by the 1998 AIA agreement.

4.2.2 Trade in goods liberalisation and facilitation under AFTA

Coverage of CEPT

The CEPT scheme for tariff reduction initially covered ten manufacturing sectors and excluded unprocessed agricultural products. There were the temporary exclusion list (TEL), sensitive list (SL) and general exclusion list (GEL) to delay or exclude products from tariff liberalisation. In September 1994 it was agreed to remove the TELs by transferring products in them to the inclusion list (IL) in five equal instalments over five years, effectively eliminating the TELs by 2000 for ASEAN6 and by 2003 for CLMV. The SL comprises unprocessed agricultural products that have been given a longer time for liberalisation, with 2010 for ASEAN6 and 2013–17 for CLMV; in particular, rice and sugar are highly sensitive for a number of ASEAN members because of national food security. The GEL covers products that are permanently excluded from liberalisation for reasons of national security, protection of human, animal or plant life and health, and articles of artistic, historic and archaeological value.

Tariff reduction/elimination schedule

Several changes were made to the initial CEPT tariff reduction/elimination schedule, some of them at the AEM in September 1994. Tariffs were initially to be reduced to the 0 per cent to 5 per cent levels over a period of fifteen years but this end-date was brought forward to 2002 for the ASEAN6 and to 2006–10 for CLMV. Initially the CEPT targeted tariff reduction to the 0 per cent to 5 per cent levels rather than zero level, as many ASEAN governments were dependent on import tariff revenues. Eventually ASEAN agreed to have zero tariff level by 2010 for ASEAN6 and by 2015 for CLMV. Further, in January 2003 it was agreed that tariffs would be completely abolished by ASEAN6 by the beginning of 2010 and by CLMV by the beginning of 2015, with some exceptions that would expire by 2018. In November 2004 the target dates for removing tariffs for priority sectors were advanced to the beginning of 2007 for ASEAN6 and 2010 for CLMV.

It is noteworthy that instead of retreating into protectionism in the wake of the AFC, the ASEAN Summit in Hanoi in December 1998, in an effort to improve FDI inflows, advanced by yet another year, to the beginning of 2002, the deadline for ASEAN6 to reduce tariffs under AFTA to 0 per cent to 5 per cent, with 90 per cent of total tariff lines accounting for 90 per cent of intra-ASEAN trade value by 2000. However, tariff liberalisation under AFTA suffered a setback when Malaysia, in trying to keep its national car project afloat in the aftermath of the AFC, asked for a delay until 2005 in the transfer of motor vehicles from its TEL to its IL.[13] ASEAN reluctantly acceded to the Malaysian request and in November 2000 the AEMM adopted a protocol allowing an AFTA signatory under certain conditions temporarily to delay the transfer of a product from its TEL into the IL, or temporarily to suspend its concession on a product already transferred into the IL, if such a transfer or concession would cause or had caused real problems.

Preferential tariff utilisation and rules of origin

Chia (2011c) noted that various surveys, including Dennis and Yusof (2003) and the Asian Development Bank (ADB) project coordinated by Kawai and Wignaraja (2011), had shown that the CEPT had a surprisingly low utilisation rate.[14] The ADB project contains a Singapore country study that also found low utilisation rates for Singapore's FTAs, including AFTA.[15] Reasons for the low utilisation rates include the low margin of preference between MFN and

[13] Malaysia failed to transfer to the Inclusion List some 218 items in the automotive sector and asked for deferment to 2004 to pre-empt import competition. Likewise, Indonesia deferred sixty-six items of agricultural products, and the Philippines deferred 192 items, mainly in agricultural products and automotive parts.

[14] Dennis and Yusof (2003) reported that Malaysia's exports under the CEPT accounted for only 2.9 per cent of its total exports to ASEAN countries. The Asian Development Bank's (2008) firm questionnaire survey for selected East Asian countries was published in Kawai and Wignaraja 2011 and found that FTA preferential tariff utilisation rates were still undesirably low.

[15] See Chia 2011c.

CEPT rates and the prevalence of non-tariff barriers. Singapore had zero differences (except for six alcoholic beverages) between the MFN and CEPT tariff rates so the CEPT provides no tariff advantages for ASEAN exporters to Singapore. But for the countries with positive average margin of preference the MFN and CEPT rates are the same for many products. In particular, electronic products and components had zero tariffs because of the Information Technology Agreement of the WTO and the duty-drawbacks in ASEAN export-processing zones. The ADB project also found that although AFTA has been in existence since 1993 many SMEs were 'unaware' of how to apply for tariff preferences, indicating that considerable outreach effort is necessary.

A further explanation for the low CEPT utilisation lies in the rules of origin (ROO) (Chia 2011c). The initial CEPT agreement contains only one sentence pertaining to ROO: 'A product shall be deemed to be originating from ASEAN member states, if at least 40 per cent of its content originates from any Member State.' This simple statement gave rise to different customs interpretations and disputes. Also, ASEAN exporters are heavily dependent on imported inputs for final processing or assembly and hence often fail to qualify under the 40 per cent content rule. The CEPT Rules of Origin and its Operational Certification Procedures have since been revised to include substantial transformation as an alternative rule for certain product sectors; a standardised method of calculating ASEAN content; a set of principles for determining cost of ASEAN origin and guidelines for costing methodologies; treatment of locally procured materials; and improved verification processes, including on-site verification.

Further problems also include a lack of consistency in treatment by customs authorities of the Form D Certificate of Origin, uncertainty on the authorised issuer of the forms, lengthy time for the forms to be issued, uncertainty on the status of tariffs, complicated payment arrangements and high cost of transport and telecommunications.

Removal of non-tariff barriers

While tariff liberalisation progressed fairly smoothly, the same cannot be said of NTBs. The 1992 CEPT agreement had provisions for elimination of quantitative restrictions (QRs) and other NTBs: all QRs on imports immediately upon application of CEPT concessions for that product and all other NTBs to be phased out within five years of the enjoyment of such concessions. The 1995 ASEAN Summit directed that all QRs be removed and NTBs eliminated beginning in January 1996. However, it took considerable time for ASEAN even to compile its NTB database: the NTBs include import quotas and anti-dumping actions as well as technical, administrative, health and safety regulations usually imposed for quality assurance and safety standards, but could also harbour protectionist intentions.

Trade facilitation measures: customs improvement

Inefficient and ambiguous customs rules, regulations and procedures and their lack of harmonisation resulting in arbitrary and corrupt application across ASEAN countries add to business transaction costs. In 1983 the customs authorities of Indonesia, Malaysia, the Philippines,

Singapore and Thailand adopted the ASEAN Code of Conduct and in 1997 the ASEAN Agreement on Customs formalised the code that aims to: establish a common system for the valuation of traded goods for customs purposes, customs classifications and tariff nomenclatures; simplify and harmonise customs procedures; and provide for the right of affected persons to appeal decisions by customs authorities.

- ASEAN decided to adopt the GATT/WTO customs valuation agreement. In 2003 the ASEAN Customs Valuation Guide and the ASEAN Post-Clearance Audit Manual were completed to ensure consistency in application of these systems among ASEAN countries.
- In August 2003 ASEAN signed the protocol adopting the ASEAN Harmonised Tariff Nomenclature (AHTN) system to provide a common system to classify and designate all goods for customs purposes – disputes over the application of the system are resolved by a technical committee whose decisions are binding. One advantage of the AHTN system is that it facilitates subsequent FTA negotiations with China, Japan, India, Australia and New Zealand.
- A Green Lane system facilitates customs clearance of goods receiving CEPT treatment and this was expanded in 1998 to cover all imports from ASEAN.
- A December 2005 agreement establishing the ASEAN Single Window commits all ASEAN countries to set up National Single Windows by 2008 for ASEAN6 and 2012 for CLMV. Under this Single Window there would

be only one point where customs data and information are submitted and processed and customs decisions are made, thus obviating the need for importers to shuttle among a number of agencies to have their shipments approved, particularly for countries with widely dispersed customs entry points such as Indonesia and the Philippines. The electronic handling of customs transactions varies among ASEAN Member States and it is time-consuming to train customs officials. There have been complaints about customs authorities in some countries deliberately putting up obstacles to circumvent obligations under the CEPT.

Trade facilitation measures: standards and mutual recognition

To minimise business transaction costs, product standards are either harmonised across ASEAN or mutual recognition arrangements (MRAs) are put in place, the latter replacing multiple with once-only testing and certification. However, common standards and even MRAs could be difficult to achieve in view of the wide development gap among ASEAN countries.

In 1997 ASEAN designated for standards harmonisation (according to international standards) by 2003 some twenty priority products,[16] followed in 1999 by an

[16] Namely, air-conditioners, refrigerators, motors and generators, telephones, radios, television sets, loudspeakers, some electronic components, condoms and medical rubber gloves.

agreement to align safety standards for seventy-one electrical appliances for commercial and household use and electromagnetic compatibility standards for ten categories of scientific and other equipment; these were completed by July 2004 but many other products remain to be harmonised. Additionally, in 1998, ASEAN adopted a framework agreement on MRAs aimed at accepting or recognising each other's conformity assessments. MRAs would obviate duplicative product testing and other forms of product compliance and thus reduce delays and costs. MRAs have been reached in the electrical and electronics, cosmetics and pharmaceutical sectors. But overall, progress on product standards harmonisation and MRAs have been very slow.

Trade facilitation measure: transportation and logistics

Transportation is crucial for the delivery of physical goods and ASEAN has taken steps to facilitate the movement of goods across its borders. Transportation development includes the development of physical infrastructure as well as removal of administrative–political and regulatory obstructions. Some businesses have complained about the high cost of land transportation in some ASEAN countries. Interstate land transport (as well as air services) is subject to bilateral agreements and regional agreements are badly needed.

- In 1995, ASEAN adopted the Singapore–Kunming Rail Link as part of the ASEAN Mekong Basin Development

Cooperation (AMBDC) programme that includes China. The route would cover 5,382 km, entailing the construction of 431 km of missing links. Other than helping trade on mainland Southeast Asia, the rail link would ease the access of the region and China to each other.

- In 1998 ASEAN moved to remove administrative–political and regulatory obstacles for the free movement of goods: it agreed that inspection certificates issued by one country for commercial vehicles be valid in the other countries and in November 2005 concluded an agreement on multimodal transport.
- Also in 1998, ASEAN concluded a framework agreement for the facilitation of transit passage of goods traded in the region: it commits the parties to ensure that goods being transported from one ASEAN country to another through a third would not be subjected to unnecessary delays, restrictions, taxation or customs inspection in the transit country. The largest transit trade in ASEAN is Thailand–Singapore through Malaysia. There were nine implementing protocols, with five protocols signed when the whole package was stalled by the Malaysia–Singapore dispute.[17]
- The 1998 Hanoi Plan of Action called for a framework and modalities by 2000 for the development of a Competitive Air Services Policy as a prelude to an ASEAN Open Sky Policy. The rapid growth of budget airlines in the region

[17] The Malaysia–Singapore border dispute arose over the continued location of the Malaysian customs, immigration and quarantine facilities inside Singapore territory instead of at the border.

was already breaking up the monopolies of ASEAN national airlines.

- In 1999 ASEAN transport ministers formalised the programme of developing the ASEAN Highway Network, approving its route configuration and with each country agreeing to upgrade to specified standards the sections running through its national territory.
- In 2002 ASEAN agreed to allow one another to deliver air cargo services to their respective territories up to one hundred tons a week. However, some countries restricted the operation of cargo services from other ASEAN countries.

4.2.3 ASEAN Industrial Cooperation (AICO)

In 1996 ASEAN also adopted a new industrial cooperation scheme (AICO) to replace earlier industrial cooperation schemes. The objective of AICO is to promote joint manufacturing between ASEAN-based companies. The qualifying criteria for AICO are a minimum of two companies in two different ASEAN countries and a minimum of 30 per cent national equity. This national equity requirement was waived following the outbreak of the AFC and the waiver remained until the end of 2005. Unlike the earlier schemes, in which ASEAN states collectively decided on product coverage, AICO allows the private sector to select the products for which to seek tariff concessions, subject to approval of AICO status by the governments immediately involved. Also, unlike earlier schemes where products enjoy exclusivity but not necessarily low tariffs, AICO products do not enjoy exclusivity but immediately enjoy AFTA end-tariff rates of 0 per cent to 5 per cent as well as local content accreditation and investment incentives offered by ASEAN national authorities. By 2002, the 0 per cent to 5 per cent tariff level for intra-ASEAN6 trade had been achieved and this removed the incentive that AICO products enjoyed. To maintain the relevance of the AICO Scheme until 2010 (when CEPT tariffs drop to zero), the scheme was amended in April 2004, removing tariffs altogether on all AICO-eligible products, reducing tariffs on AICO products to zero (and 1 per cent for the Philippines) by the beginning of 2005, except for Vietnam (reduced by the beginning of 2006).

Most of the AICO applicants are in the electronic and automotive sectors and involve well-known electronic companies, such as Denso, Sony, Matsushita, Yamaha, Samsung, and automotive companies, such as Toyota, Honda, Volvo, Isuzu, Nissan, Ford and Mitsubishi. Among ASEAN countries, only Indonesia, Malaysia, the Philippines and Thailand have participated extensively in AICO; Singapore and Vietnam are each involved in only three projects, with two in electronics and one in automotive components (Severino 2006). As of February 2007, the AICO Scheme approved 140 regional supply projects in ASEAN countries alone, centred on MNCs from both Asian and non-Asian countries. AICO has successfully promoted production networks in automobile and electronics industries, by reducing the preferential tariff rate to 0 per cent to 5 per cent and liberalising equity restrictions for foreign investors.

4.2.4 Trade in services liberalisation under AFAS

To improve the efficiency and competitiveness of ASEAN services, ASEAN concluded the Framework Agreement on ASEAN Services (AFAS) in December 1995 providing for the elimination of discriminatory measures, market access limitations and other restrictions on trade in services.

ASEAN member states who are members of the WTO[18] are already committed to services liberalisation under the General Agreement on Trade in Services (GATS) in addition to unilateral services liberalisation. Does AFAS have value added? There are advantages in negotiating regional services trade agreements. First, services are an increasingly important part of ASEAN national economies. Second, integrating the services sector is an essential component of regional economic integration elsewhere such as NAFTA and NAFTA-type bilateral FTAs. Third, an ASEAN-wide agreement will help lock in the unilateral liberalisation measures already undertaken by member states. Fourth, negotiating services liberalisation at the regional level will help hold back domestic protectionist pressures and prepare the member states for further services liberalisation at the WTO as well as services liberalisation in ASEAN and bilateral FTAs.

AFAS aims at liberalising trade in services beyond commitments in the GATS and so improve the efficiency and competitiveness of ASEAN service suppliers. Services

[18] As of 2002, ASEAN membership of WTO comprised only ASEAN6 and Myanmar. Cambodia acceded to WTO in 2003 followed by Vietnam in 2007 and Laos in 2012.

negotiations under AFAS follow the WTO mode of request and offer, which does not encourage 'offers' from those not wanting to open up to foreign competition and no agreement is reached until all members agree to the totality of the package offered. ASEAN later modified the negotiating approach to the more flexible 'ASEAN minus X' formula to accommodate member countries unable to move at the same pace: under the new formula, two or more ASEAN countries can start to negotiate services trade liberalisation for specific sectors/sub-sectors, while other members could join at a later stage.

Services trade liberalisation involves four modes of supply – mode 1 (cross-border supply), mode 2 (consumption abroad), mode 3 (commercial presence) and mode 4 (movement of natural persons). The general reluctance to liberalise services under mode 3 and mode 4 led to modifications in subsequent services negotiations, which resulted in liberalisation of all limitations for mode 1 and mode 2 but only progressive liberalisation for mode 3 and mode 4.

AFAS requires negotiations to be conducted sector by sector. Services trade liberalisation is achieved through rounds of negotiations, with each round resulting in a package of commitments by ASEAN member states in each agreed sector/sub-sector and mode of supply. Countries have so far negotiated and agreed on eight packages of commitments under AFAS that cover business services, professional services, construction, distribution, education, environmental services, healthcare, maritime transport, telecommunications and tourism. ASEAN has also concluded MRAs for professional services covering engineering, architecture, accountancy, surveying, medical practitioners, dental practitioners, nursing services and tourism professionals.

Services liberalisation under AFAS has not kept pace with goods liberalisation under AFTA. Assessment made in the mid-term review of the Hanoi Plan of Action suggested that there were still substantial barriers to integration in services, progress in negotiations has been slow and indicative offers have been slow in coming. At the AEMM in September 2005 ministers declared 2015 as the end-date for liberalisation of all services sectors. Many negotiations are extremely cautious either because of their uncertainty about the impact of liberalisation and fear of the loss of regulatory control in some service sectors (such as financial services) or because of the power of domestic special interests.

4.2.5 *Investment liberalisation, facilitation and promotion under the AIA*

FDI inflows have played a crucial role in the development, industrialisation and resource development of ASEAN economies. FDI has played a particularly important role in the switch to an outward development strategy and in linking with regional production networks and global supply chains.

In December 1987 ASEAN concluded an agreement on the promotion and protection of investments, and in 1996 updated this with a protocol. In 1998 ASEAN concluded the

ASEAN Investment Area (AIA) agreement aimed at providing a policy environment to facilitate the free flows of investment and participation in global and regional production networks. The AIA grants national treatment to ASEAN investors by 2010 and to non-ASEAN investors by 2020, with some exceptions specified in the TEL, SL and GEL. A 2001 protocol advanced the date for full realisation of the AIA to 2010 for ASEAN6 and 2015 for CLMV, and removed the differential treatment between ASEAN and non-ASEAN investors. Critics had argued the distinction did not make sense since foreign investors are mostly from non-ASEAN countries. Additionally, each ASEAN country is to grant all other ASEAN countries, on an MFN basis, the investment privileges that it would accord to non-ASEAN countries under bilateral agreements. Sectoral coverage of the AIA includes manufacturing, agriculture, fisheries, forestry and mining, and services incidental to those sectors. ASEAN6 and Myanmar agreed to phase out their TELs in manufacturing by 2003; Vietnam, Cambodia and Laos by 2010. Malaysia and Singapore did not have TELs. According to the mid-term review of the Hanoi Plan of Action, some countries faced difficulties in drawing up the TEL and SL for services that are incidental to manufacturing, agriculture, fishery, forestry and mining. The TELs and SLs for services were submitted only in 2002. The extent and type of barriers to investment are indicated by the length and content of the various TELs, SLs and GELs.

The AIA could be criticised for its long exclusion lists, although there have been improvements in that direction. In 2003, the sectoral coverage was expanded from services incidental to other economic sectors to include services such as education, healthcare, telecommunications, tourism, banking and finance, insurance, trading, e-commerce, distribution and logistics, transportation and warehousing, and professional services such as accounting, engineering and advertising. The deadlines for phasing out the TELs in manufacturing were brought forward to January 2003 for the ASEAN6 and Myanmar and to January 2010 for Cambodia, Laos and Vietnam. The deadlines for phasing out the TELs in agriculture, fishery, forestry, mining and related services are 2010 for the ASEAN6 and Cambodia, 2013 for Vietnam and 2015 for Laos and Myanmar. The GEL consists of industries and investment measures that are not open to FDI for reasons of national security, public morals, public health and environmental protection. As with services liberalisation, the 'ASEAN minus X' formula was introduced.

To improve the investment climate, the AIA agreement calls for reduction/elimination of regulations and conditions impeding investment flows and investment project operation, such as ensuring transparency and consistency in application and interpretation of their investment laws, regulations and administrative procedures. ASEAN countries are to exchange their action plans on facilitating, promoting and liberalising inflows of investments. The ASEAN Secretariat compiled and published the plans.

The AIA also contains an investment promotion programme, which includes joint investment promotion missions to target countries, creation of investment websites and databases and timely publication of investment information. Reports are that the joint investment promotion missions failed in their objective of attracting FDI into ASEAN as a destination, as national investment agencies focused on attracting FDI into their own respective territories.

4.2.6 Assessment of economic integration up to the end of the AFTA period

A common yardstick to measure the extent of economic integration achieved is to look at what happens to intra-regional trade. For ASEAN, intra-ASEAN trade share grew from 17 per cent in 1990 (pre-AFTA) to 25 per cent in 2011, representing a significant improvement in intra-regional trade share. However, the improved trade share may not necessarily be attributable to the implementation of the CEPT. As noted earlier, CEPT tariff preference utilisation rates have been consistently low in a number of studies, belying the negotiators' claim that FTAs were intended to benefit businesses. However, notwithstanding the low CEPT preferential tariff utilisation rates, it could still be argued that removal of some NTBs and improvements in customs administration and in trade logistics as a result of AFTA have promoted intra-ASEAN trade. Critics will point out that a 25 per cent intra-ASEAN trade share is still significantly lower than that achieved by regional groupings such as NAFTA and EU.

More importantly, increasing the intra-ASEAN trade share has not been the raison d'être of ASEAN economic integration as ascertained from various statements issued at Summit and Ministerial meetings and from comments of various ASEAN leaders and officials. The main raison d'être of ASEAN economic integration appears to be maintaining ASEAN's competitiveness in attracting FDI from external sources and from within ASEAN. It is difficult to determine the impact of AFTA, AFAS and AIA on the investment decisions of foreign multinationals. The AIA includes the goal of joint investment promotion by ASEAN countries in missions to Japan, Europe and the USA but, as noted earlier, these have not been an unqualified success. ASEAN's share of global FDI destined for the developing world has been declining in recent decades but this is mainly attributable to the rise of China as an investment destination as well as the impact of the AFC. Intra-ASEAN investments have been dominated by investments from the more advanced countries of Singapore, Malaysia and Thailand, and in recent years CLMV as well as Indonesia have attracted sizeable investments from the more advanced ASEAN countries, with regional economic integration playing a significant role in improving the investment climate in CLMV.

Progress in economic integration in the AFTA period could also be ascertained by analysing the success or otherwise in implementing the various integration measures. The largest integration effort has been directed at the goods market, and here ASEAN has largely kept its commitments, even advancing the end-dates of its tariff reduction/elimination schedules. AICO could also be deemed a success from the perspective of its use by foreign multinationals in the automotive and electronics sectors. However, the removal of NTBs and improving trade logistics have a more spotty record and this is a concern for businesses seeking certainty, efficiency and cost effectiveness in supply chains. ASEAN had not adopted common criteria for identifying NTBs let alone starting to dismantle them. The AHTN has been successfully implemented and this has facilitated subsequent negotiations of the various ASEAN+1 FTAs. But customs processes remain slow and unpredictable, with stories of corruption; common product standards have been agreed for only twenty priority product groups, safety standards for seventy-one types of electrical appliances and ten electromagnetic compatibility standards. Other measures are still works-in-progress, including services sector liberalisation, passage of goods in transit, development of transport connectivity and improvement of trade logistics, and implementation of MRAs on product groups and on professional qualifications.

The 2001 mid-term review of the Hanoi Plan of Action highlighted some of the implementation problems.

- First, weak commitments to some of the decisions to promote liberalisation and cooperation programmes, possibly owing to poor awareness of the benefits of liberalisation. For example, basic information necessary for implementation was not always forthcoming or the submission of information was delayed. Weak commitment was also reflected in the low level of representation at negotiations and meetings, resulting in the inability to make critical decisions at such meetings.
- Second, slowness in implementing decisions that have been taken owing to the need to consider national interests of all parties concerned. Such intra-country consultations are

necessary but time-consuming to resolve, particularly where there are perceived conflicts between ASEAN commitments and the national interest.

- Third, new legislation and changes to existing legislation by member countries to accommodate the requirements of ASEAN decisions can be time-consuming.
- Fourth, in some cases, there are delays in implementation owing to a lack of appropriate and sufficient technical capacity for implementation.
- Fifth, some of the activities of ASEAN need to involve the private sector and such consultations have to be initiated.
- Sixth, there were inadequate financial resources to support ASEAN's programmes.

Rodolfo Severino, a former ASEAN Secretary General and hence an insider of the ASEAN integration process, concluded that regional economic integration seems to have become stuck in framework agreements, work programmes and master plans (Severino 2006: 344). Apart from tariff reduction and elimination, other measures where ASEAN has fallen short are due to several reasons.

- First, NTBs are largely opaque and hard to identify and even more difficult to remove, as they are often subtle instruments of protectionism and rent-seeking.
- Second, services are more sensitive than trade in goods. For example, liberalising transportation services would expose to greater competition national airlines, shipping lines and land transport companies, many of which are state-owned or crony-owned and used to protection by the state. Trans-boundary transport

arrangements can also be held hostage to political disputes or pressures.

- Third, streamlining customs operations and coordinating them regionally may require the overhaul of entire cultures at some national customs authorities. Regulatory bodies may have to give up a measure of their authority in order to harmonise product standards with other ASEAN countries and give recognition to those countries' certificates of compliance with regulations. Governments will have to ensure that companies adjust to ASEAN norms and abandon the standards that they have adhered to for years.
- Fourth, ASEAN has no compliance or enforcement mechanisms and a failure to implement carries no sanctions, as is the case with the EU. The ASEAN Secretariat has no power to enforce agreements or the authority even to expose non-compliance with them.
- Fifth, a fundamental problem is that most ASEAN governments do not feel a sufficient identification of the national interest with regional economic integration. Most ASEAN companies do not see how their businesses benefit from such integration – for example, Indonesian firms not only failed to recognise the benefits of an integrated regional market, but also lacked confidence in their ability to compete even in their own domestic market. Most firms, and thus national governments, place much more value on extra-ASEAN markets in Europe, America, Japan and China. The result is that the governments feel no pressure from ASEAN businesses to move faster on regional economic

integration. The strongest advocates of ASEAN integration are, in fact, foreign business groups such as those of the USA (through the US–ASEAN Business Council) and Japan (through Keidanren, the Japanese Federation of Economic Organisations) – this reinforces the perception that, more than ASEAN companies it is the MNCs that benefit from AFTA and other measures to integrate the ASEAN economy. Only a handful of ASEAN companies participate in AICO.

Chapter 5

The AEC and its economic effects

ASEAN Community Building comprises the ASEAN Economic Community (AEC), complemented by the ASEAN Political-Security Community (APSC) and the ASEAN Socio-Cultural Community (ASCC).

5.1 Rationale and process towards the AEC

At the November 2002 ASEAN Summit it was decided to move on to the next stage of regional economic integration. According to Severino the term AEC was coined by then Singapore Prime Minister Goh Chok Tong to evoke the idea of the EEC, as he and a few other ASEAN leaders were deeply concerned over the weakened ability of ASEAN countries to attract FDI in the aftermath of the AFC as well as the rise of China and India as competing destinations for investment.[1] For ASEAN to meet these challenges it had to deepen

[1] Severino (2006: 344) maintains the term ASEAN Economic Community evokes the European Economic Community (EEC), created in 1957, which eventually evolved into the European Union (EU). It does not mean that ASEAN intended to achieve the level of Europe's political and economic integration; rather it indicated that ASEAN did seek to project itself as moving towards a degree of market integration that would make that integrated market large and diverse enough to be an attractive option for investors, and that ASEAN would be proceeding faster on the road to integration than previously.

economic integration to persuade investors that ASEAN was serious about regional economic integration and clear about its objective. Specifically, investors had to be persuaded that ASEAN, when integrated, would have a prospective domestic market that could compete with China. The AEC would have almost half of China's population and would equal China's GDP size.

The Bali Summit in 2003 issued the Declaration of ASEAN Concord II to create the AEC. The AEC is based on the 1997 ASEAN Vision 2020,[2] calling for a stable, prosperous and highly competitive ASEAN economic region in which there is free flow of goods, services, investment and a freer flow of capital, equitable economic development and reduced poverty and socio-economic disparities in the year 2020. This was to be achieved by transforming ASEAN into a single market and production base, as a more dynamic and stronger segment of the global supply chain. For this ASEAN would set up new mechanisms and measures to strengthen the implementation of its existing economic initiatives (including AFTA, negotiations on AFAS, and AIA); facilitate movement of business persons, skilled labour and talents; and ensure expeditious and legally binding resolution of any economic disputes. It called for implementation of the recommendations of the High Level Task Force (HLTF) on ASEAN Economic Integration.[3]

[2] ASEAN Vision 2020 was agreed by ASEAN Heads of State in Kuala Lumpur on 15 December 1997.

[3] Two months before the November 2002 Phnom Penh Summit, ASEAN Economic Ministers had agreed to form a High Level Task Force on ASEAN Economic Integration to recommend measures for deepening

The HLTF had recommended the following.

- Accelerate current ASEAN economic integration programmes, laying down clear deadlines for specific measures in the areas of tariffs, non-tariff measures, customs, standards, services, investments, intellectual property rights and finance.
- Designate eleven priority sectors for accelerated integration, with the coverage of each sector broad enough to account for a substantial portion of intra-ASEAN trade (identified as agro-based products; air transport; automotives; e-ASEAN; electronics; fisheries; healthcare; rubber-based products; textiles and apparel; tourism; and wood-based products).
- Adopt an 'ASEAN minus X' formula in integrating the eleven priority sectors – that is, two or more ASEAN members may initiate and participate in intra-ASEAN economic arrangements, while other ASEAN members may join in when they are ready to do so.
- Establish new institutional mechanisms – advisory mechanism in each ASEAN country to help solve operational problems encountered by business firms and people, a legal unit on trade disputes in the ASEAN Secretariat, a compliance monitoring body for peer adjudication of such disputes and an impartial dispute settlement mechanism.

the region's economic integration beyond AFTA. This was in response to the McKinsey study commissioned by ASEAN that had concluded that ASEAN had great economic promise and potentially large market but was losing out to others as an investment destination because of its market fragmentation.

In November 2004 the Vientiane Action Programme (VAP) was adopted, laying down goals and strategies for bringing the ASEAN Community to reality. The ASEAN Framework Agreement for the Integration of Priority Sectors formalised the measures agreed upon in the VAP, with eleven protocols for the eleven priority sectors.[4] The AEC Blueprint, outlining the various measures and strategic schedules for implementation, was adopted in late 2007.

5.2 Benefits of the AEC

The economic literature lists several benefits of economic integration, including an enlarged market with economies of scale and scope, improved resource allocation with free movement of factors of production, improved resource pools with inflows of capital and labour, and competition leading to improved efficiency and innovation. Plummer and Chia (2009) discuss the benefits from the establishment of the AEC for various ASEAN stakeholders (government, business, labour, consumers) and these are outlined below.

5.2.1 *Benefits from liberalisation of trade in goods and services*

The AEC expands, deepens and modernises the coverage of ASEAN economic integration. The creation of a single market and production base should allow ASEAN to benefit from economies of scale and efficiency in production network

[4] A twelfth priority sector, logistics, was added later.

processes, while other aspects of the AEC will boost competitiveness, strengthen ASEAN institutions and improve the region's socio-economic environment.

The elimination of intra-ASEAN tariffs and non-tariff barriers will boost intra-ASEAN trade and in the process have positive effects on economic growth and employment, result in more efficient allocation of resources and thus gains in productivity, encouraging foreign and domestic investments, lower business costs, increase economic competitiveness, and lower consumer prices and widen consumer choice. Removal of barriers to trade (tariffs, NTBs) and trade facilitation measures (including transport and communications connectivity) will encourage the growth of production networks in ASEAN and plug ASEAN and individual ASEAN countries into global supply chains.

The services sector becomes increasingly important as ASEAN countries move up the ladder of economic development, for three reasons. First, consumption of services such as education, healthcare, financial services and public sector services are income-elastic and rise as per capita incomes rise. Second, services constitute an important input in the production of primary commodities and manufacturing, and the efficient provision of services inputs affects the competitiveness of the other economic sectors of the economy. Third, services facilitate trade and enhance competitiveness: an efficient services sector facilitates participation in regional production networks and global supply chains.

Behind-the-border policies such as competition policy and intellectual property rights (IPR) protection, as well as infrastructure and spatial connectivity, affect competition and ASEAN competitiveness. Implementation of a sound competition policy improves economic efficiency and income distribution. Consumer protection improves living standards, particularly for low income households. Better IPR protection encourages technology transfer, local innovations and protection of Southeast Asia's indigenous technologies and property rights. Adequate transport and communications infrastructure lower the costs of distribution and communication and these are important cost factors in trading operations and also facilitate movement of people across ASEAN. Free trade areas lead to market and factor openings and formalise economic relations with partner countries, reducing business costs and market uncertainties.

5.2.2 *Benefits from liberalisation of investment and skilled labour flows*

As discussed earlier, ASEAN countries' successful economic performance in the 1980s and 1990s was due in large part to their export-led and FDI-led development model. Free movement of goods and services needs to be complemented and supplemented by free movement of investment and skilled labour.

FDI brings benefits of financial resources for fixed investment as well as technological and managerial know-how, participation in regional production networks and global supply chains, resulting in improved efficiency in production and marketing. FDI flows can be classified as market-seeking (both market size and growth potential), efficiency-seeking (affecting production, procurement and distribution cost competitiveness), resource-seeking and infrastructure development. The increasingly integrated ASEAN market and its robust growth have become increasingly attractive for foreign MNCs. Some ASEAN countries, such as Indonesia, Malaysia, Myanmar and Vietnam, are also resource rich, while several ASEAN countries have abundant low-wage labour, giving them a comparative advantage in labour-intensive industries. General factors contributing to a favourable investment climate include: political and economic stability; large market size and favourable economic prospects; available educated, well-disciplined low-wage labour; well-developed soft and hard infrastructure; and a FDI-friendly policy regime. The ASEAN Comprehensive Investment Area (ACIA) adopted in March 2012 builds on the earlier AIA and has the four components of FDI: liberalisation, facilitation, promotion and protection. An improved investment climate resulting from implementation of ACIA will encourage inflows of FDI.

Mobility of skilled labour (including professionals) is essential for effective implementation of services liberalisation and FDI liberalisation as well as for deeper economic integration. A free flow of skilled labour will increase ASEAN's attractiveness for foreign MNCs, particularly as it meets their need for intra-corporate transfer of management and technical personnel. Easier movement of ASEAN professionals within the region will facilitate people-to-people contact and enable transfers of know-how, experiences and best practices.

5.2.3 *Benefits of financial and capital market development*

Since the AFC, developing financial resilience has been a high priority for ASEAN countries. This has led to reforms of domestic financial and banking systems, better macroeconomic management and accumulation of foreign exchange reserves to hedge against external shocks. The benefits of these moves were seen when the USA-originated financial crisis erupted in 2008 and the ASEAN region suffered very limited financial contagion. Instead, the negative impact was manifested primarily in the sharp decline in exports to OECD economies.

Financial and capital market development is seen as providing more efficient markets to finance trade, investment and corporate development in ASEAN countries. For Singapore, financial services is a growth industry as well, as its financial centre contributes significantly to GDP growth and to high-wage employment. Cooperation in ASEAN and in ASEAN+3 (that is, including also China, Japan and South Korea) has resulted in several financial initiatives such as the Chiang Mai Initiative, the Asian Bond Market and the Regional Surveillance Mechanism.

5.2.4 *Benefits from narrowing the development gap*

ASEAN economies are characterised by wide economic diversity in factor endowments, economic structures and levels of economic development, as discussed earlier. Specifically, the wide development gap is manifested in the huge differences in per capita income between Brunei–Singapore at one end and CLMV at the other. It is generally accepted that a wide development gap would lead to negative spillover effects between rich and poor neighbourhoods as well as hinder consensus building and the speed of progress towards the AEC, APSC and ASCC.

When CLMV joined ASEAN in 1995–9, there was concern that a two-tiered ASEAN had emerged, as CLMV countries were doubly handicapped by being less developed than ASEAN6 and by being transitional economies, thus facing greater difficulties in integrating with ASEAN and implementing the various ASEAN agreements. It was recognised that 'special and differential treatment' would have to be accorded CLMV in terms of delayed timelines and flexibilities in meeting ASEAN liberalisation commitments, and in provision of development and technical assistance from ASEAN6 (as well as from ASEAN Dialogue Partners) targeted for CLMV. It should be noted that ASEAN did not adopt the EU's structural funds and cohesion fund model for its less-developed regions.[5] Instead, the Initiative for ASEAN

[5] The Structural Funds and Cohesion Fund are financial tools to implement the EU's regional policy. They aim to reduce regional disparities in income, wealth and opportunities, and the poorer regions of the EU receive most of the support, although all EU regions are eligible for funding. Funding priorities include: modernising economic structures, creating sustainable jobs and economic growth, research and innovation, environmental protection and risk prevention. Investment in infrastructure also retains an important role, especially in the least-developed regions. The Cohesion Fund is used for the environment and trans-European transport networks and applies to member states with a

Integration (IAI) is the key policy instrument to provide economic and technical development assistance to CLMV countries, embodying also the transfer of know-how, development experience and best practices from the more advanced ASEAN countries.

5.2.5 *Quantifying the benefits of the AEC from CGE modelling*

How could we quantify the effects of the AEC? Doing so is no mean feat, given the complicated nature of the AEC programme. The empirical trade literature estimating the effects of regional trade agreements is large but is often focused on liberalisation of tariff barriers, which tend to be the easiest trade barriers to identify: they are transparent, are expressed in percentage terms and tariff data are easily available. However, as noted above, the AEC is less about liberalisation of tariff barriers than about non-tariff and behind-the-border measures. This complicates analysis considerably.

Computable General Equilibrium (CGE) models have become the most popular tool for estimating the effects of regional integration. A CGE model includes international market linkages using mathematical modelling and real-world data from a benchmark year. The mathematical

gross national income (GNI) of less than 90 per cent of the EU average, thus covering all twelve new member states as well as Greece, Portugal and Spain. The Structural Funds and the Cohesion Fund account for the majority of EU spending in the EU budget, which is funded mainly from import duties under the common external tariffs, sugar levies and the value added tax.

modelling is based on a set of neoclassical economic assumptions about the motivation of agents in the economy, market structure, consumer preferences, production technology and market equilibrium conditions. These assumptions are coded in mathematical functions and equations, which contain parameters that capture important behavioural relationships. In a CGE model, most of these parameters are elasticities (that is, they measure the responsiveness of one variable to changes in another) or share parameters such as the share of consumption demand in aggregate demand. Some of these parameters will have known values, while others will have to be calibrated in the mathematical model with real-world data. Calibration is a step in CGE analysis when values are selected to make the CGE model's output agree with real-world data from the benchmark year.

A CGE model essentially captures demand and supply in each sector and the linkages among sectors. The model has exogenous variables (that is, variables that have given values determined outside the model) and endogenous variables (that is, variables that are solved within the model). In the analysis of an FTA, the exogenous variables typically correspond to the trade policy variables, elasticities and share parameters. The rest of the variables in a CGE model of an FTA are endogenous, including prices, import and export volumes, household income, tariff revenue, consumer surplus, producer surplus and so on.

A CGE modelling exercise, incorporating assumptions on complete elimination of tariffs and NTBs, liberalisation of five service sectors, AEC-induced changes in FDI and a 5 per cent reduction in trade costs, as well as other

Table 5.1 *Welfare gains of the ASEAN Economic Community, 2015*

	ASEAN Free Trade Area	ASEAN Economic Community	ASEAN Free Trade Area	ASEAN Economic Community
	US$ billion (2004 price)		Percentage of baseline GDP	
Brunei	0.2	0.5	2.6	7.0
Indonesia	1.0	27.6	0.2	6.2
Malaysia	2.7	5.7	1.4	3.0
Philippines	0.9	4.5	0.6	3.2
Singapore	2.6	15.1	1.6	9.7
Thailand	1.6	12.2	0.6	4.9
Cambodia	0.3	0.6	2.7	6.3
Laos	0.0	0.2	0.6	3.6
Myanmar	0.0	0.6	0.3	4.4
Vietnam	0.9	2.4	1.1	2.8
ASEAN total	**10.1**	**69.4**	**0.8**	**5.3**

Source: Michael G. Plummer and Siow Yue Chia (eds.), *Realizing the ASEAN Economic Community: A Comprehensive Assessment* (Singapore: Institute of Southeast Asian Studies, 2009), ch. 2.

quantitative exercises undertaken for the Plummer and Chia (2009) study, yielded the following results for the AEC scenario (Petri et al. 2012) summarised in Table 5.1.

- ASEAN economic welfare under the AEC should rise by 5.3 per cent or US$69 billion relative to the baseline – that is, more than six times the effect estimated for AFTA. All ASEAN countries benefit, although some benefit more than others, either absolutely or relative to GDP size.
- To estimate the direct effects of behind-the-border measures and best practices spread by means of the AEC, the

projections suggest that competition policy alone could raise per capita GDP by 26 per cent to 38 per cent in ASEAN6, including 8 per cent to 14 per cent owing to FDI attracted by policy reform. And, by creating opportunities for production networks and spreading best practices that boost productivity, AEC should help CLMV converge with ASEAN6.

- The net benefits of the AEC would be larger than the estimated 5.3 per cent increase in ASEAN economic welfare, owing to gains that have not been quantified by the CGE model (including those related to competition policy noted above). These include: first, lower cost of capital owing to freer movement of capital and improved financial systems; second, efficiency gains from freer movement of skilled labour; third, greater macroeconomic stability owing to the conservative macroeconomic policies necessary to support the AEC.

A cautionary note on the modelling results is called for. The results are sensitive to data reliability, model specifications and its underlying assumptions. For example, trade data on Singapore available to modellers refer to the country's total exports, inclusive of the substantial share of entrepôt exports that cannot qualify for ASEAN preferential tariffs under the CEPT and the ASEAN Trade in Goods Agreement (ATIGA). Further, an underlying assumption on the benefits of free trade in goods is that businesses would fully utilise the ASEAN preferential tariffs offered. Yet a six-country study coordinated by Kawai and Wignaraja (2011) shows that actual utilisation of FTA tariff preferences fell far short of that, with utilisation rates ranging from 45.1 per cent in the Philippines to 17.3 per cent in Singapore. This is not necessarily a bad thing from an economic point of view, as firms will seek preferential access only if the gains are greater than the bureaucratic costs. If they are not utilising preferences under AFTA and ATIGA because it is expensive to do so, this would suggest a problem. However, it may also be because ASEAN economies already have liberal regimes – suggesting little gain under AFTA and ATIGA and beyond MFN – and, hence, the potential gains would be small. As most intra-regional trade is in electronics and petroleum products where MFN tariffs are extremely low in ASEAN economies, we might suggest that it is not a problem from an economic perspective. Nevertheless, it still constitutes a drawback for the CGE modelling.

5.3 The AEC: component pillars and core elements

Initially, the AEC was to be realised by 2020, but in January 2007 this was brought forward to 2015 (with a longer timeline of 2018–20 for CLMV). The AEC has often been inappropriately compared to the EU Single Market in the media. But it is neither a customs union (with common external tariff) nor a full common market (with free mobility of capital and labour and some policy harmonisation). Instead, it has four pillars that aim to 'transform ASEAN into a single market and production base, a highly competitive economic region, a region of equitable economic development, and a region fully integrated into the global economy'.[6] Table 5.2 sets out the four pillars and core elements of the AEC.

[6] ASEAN Secretariat 2008.

Table 5.2 *AEC Blueprint: four pillars and core elements*

Pillars	Core elements
A. Single market and production base	A1. Free flow of goods: 9 strategic approaches
	A2. Free flow of services: 3 strategic approaches
	A3. Free flow of investment: 5 strategic approaches
	A4. Freer flow of capital: 7 strategic approaches
	A5. Free flow of skilled labour
	A6. Priority integration sectors
	A7. Food, agriculture and forestry
B. Competitive economic region	B1. Competition policy
	B2. Consumer protection
	B3. Intellectual property rights
	B4. Infrastructure development: 10 strategic approaches
	B5. Taxation
	B6. E-commerce
C. Equitable economic development	C1. SME development
	C2. Initiative for ASEAN Integration
D. Integration into global economy	D1. Coherent approach towards external economic relations
	D2. Enhanced participation in global supply networks

Source: ASEAN Secretariat, *The ASEAN Economic Community Blueprint* (Jakarta: ASEAN Secretariat, 2008).

The single market and production base involves:

- Free flow of goods (under AFTA in 1993 and under ATIGA in 2010) with reduction and elimination of tariffs and NTBs, liberalising the rules of origin, customs integration, establishing the ASEAN Single Window, and standards and conformance.

- Free flow of services with implementation of AFAS, MRAs and cooperation on financial services.
- Free flow of investment with implementation of AIA (in 1998) and ACIA (in March 2012) with investment liberalisation, facilitation, promotion and protection.
- Freer (not free) flow of capital with a strengthening of ASEAN capital market development and integration, and facilitating measures on foreign direct and portfolio investment, and current account transactions. In April 2009 the Implementation Plan to promote the development of an integrated ASEAN capital market was endorsed. An enlarged US$120 billion swap arrangement under the Chiang Mai Initiative Multilateralized (CMIM) was finalised in December 2009. In line with the road map of the Asian Bond Market Initiative (ABMI) there are continued efforts to promote the issuing of and demand for local currency denominated bonds; also the establishment of the Credit Guarantee and Investment Facility (CGIF) aimed at supporting the issuance of local currency denominated bonds in the region.
- Free flow of skilled labour (unskilled and semi-skilled labour flows remain a highly sensitive issue). It entails completing MRAs for major professional services and developing core competencies (concordance of skills and qualifications) for jobs/occupational skills in services sectors. Several MRAs have been signed to date.

- Enhancement of ASEAN trade and competitiveness in food, agriculture and forestry sectors and improvement in regional food security. ASEAN established the ASEAN Integrated Food Security Framework and its medium-term Strategic Plan of Action on ASEAN food security.
- Priority integration sectors: significant progress has been made covering agro-based, automotive, electronics, fisheries, rubber-based, textiles and apparel, wood-based, air transport, e-ASEAN/ICT, healthcare, logistics and tourism.

5.4 The AEC Blueprint and its implementation

The 2008 AEC Blueprint sets out the measures to be taken and the schedule for the biennial years from 2008 to 2015.[7] In April 2009 ASEAN Leaders signed the Declaration on the Roadmap for the ASEAN Community (2009–15) and agreed on the accelerated timetable for realisation of the AEC. In April 2012, against a background of great uncertainty and bleak outlook for the global economy, ASEAN committed to redoubling efforts and setting priority activities and concrete key actions to realise the AEC by 2015. The schedule for the reduction/elimination of tariffs and NTBs is shown in Table 5.3.

The following discusses the implementation of the various core elements and strategic schedules in the AEC Blueprint.

[7] *Ibid.*

Table 5.3 *AEC: tariff and NTB reduction/elimination schedule*

	2008–9	2010–11	2012–13	2014–15
Tariff reduction	Complete tariff reduction to 0 per cent to 5 per cent for all IL products for Laos and Myanmar (2008)	Complete tariff reduction to 0 per cent to 5 per cent for all IL products for Cambodia (2010)		
Tariff elimination	Integrate products outside CEPT Scheme according to CEPT Agreement (2008)			
	Eliminate import duties on 60 per cent of all IL products except for those phased in from SL and Highly Sensitive List (HSL) for Laos and Myanmar (2008)	Eliminate import duties on 60 per cent of all IL products except for those phased in from SL and HSL for Cambodia (2010)		

Table 5.3 (*cont.*)

	2008–9	2010–11	2012–13	2014–15
	Eliminate import duties on 80 per cent of all IL products except for those phased in from SL and HSL for ASEAN6 (2007)	Eliminate import duties on 80 per cent of all IL products except for those phased in from SL and HSL for Vietnam (2010)	Eliminate import duties on 80 per cent of all IL products except for those phased in from SL and HSL for Laos and Myanmar (2012)	
		Eliminate tariffs on all products, except for those phased in from SL and HSL for ASEAN6 (2010)		Eliminate tariffs on all products, except for those phased in from SL and HSL for CLMV 2015 with flexibility on some sensitive products up to 2018
	Eliminate import duties on products in the Priority Integration Sectors (PIS) for ASEAN6 (2007)		Eliminate import duties on products in the PIS for CLMV (2012)	

Elimination of duties for first and second tranche of ICT products for CLMV according to the Framework Agreement on e-ASEAN (2008 for first tranche and 2009 for second tranche)	Elimination of duties for third tranche ICT products for CLMV according to Framework Agreement on e-ASEAN (2010)		
	Reduce tariffs on SL products to 0 per cent to 5 per cent for ASEAN6 (2010)	Reduce tariffs on SL products to 0 per cent to 5 per cent for Vietnam (2013). For sugar, Vietnam shall reduce tariffs to 0 per cent to 5 per cent by 2010	Complete phase in of remaining products in SL into CEPT Scheme and reduce tariffs on them to 0 per cent to 5 per cent (2015 Laos and Myanmar, 2017 Cambodia)
	Complete tariff reduction schedule for HSL to the agreed end-date		

Table 5.3 (*cont.*)

	2008–9	2010–11	2012–13	2014–15
NTB elimination	Abide by the commitment of a standstill and rollback on NTBs effective immediately			
	Enhance transparency by abiding with the Protocol on Notification Procedure and setting up an effective Surveillance Mechanism			
		Eliminate NTBs for ASEAN5 (2010)	Eliminate NTBs for Philippines (2012)	Eliminate NTBs for CLMV (2015) with flexibility to 2018 for some sensitive products

Source: ASEAN Secretariat, *The ASEAN Economic Community Blueprint* (Jakarta: ASEAN Secretariat, 2008).

5.4.1 Trade in goods liberalisation: tariffs, NTBs and Rules of Origin

Tariffs

From January 2010, all tariffs for CEPT Inclusion Lists of ASEAN6 have been eliminated, representing 99 per cent of ASEAN total tariff lines and the average tariff is down to 0.9. For CLMV countries, tariff levels were down to the 0 per cent to 5 per cent level by 2010 and will be eliminated by 2015. Tariff eliminations/reductions are largely on track for products in the CEPT ILs, which cover 99.3 per cent of all tariff lines for Myanmar, 98.3 per cent for Cambodia, 97.5 per cent for Singapore, 96.6 per cent for Vietnam, 95.2 per cent for Laos, 94 per cent for Thailand, 92.9 per cent for Brunei, 87.4 per cent for Malaysia, 78.4 per cent for Indonesia and 79.6 per cent for the Philippines. The percentages refer to tariff lines and actual value of tariff-free intra-ASEAN trade for each country is not available. In addition to the CEPT ILs, there are the Sensitive List and General Exclusion List. It is difficult to eliminate tariffs in the Sensitive List, particularly on rice and sugar.

NTBs

With the elimination of most tariffs, NTBs emerge as a serious trade impediment. ASEAN is in the process of stocktaking and updating the NTMs database. It is a difficult process to identify all the NTMs in each country (and at the sub-country level), especially as not all NTMs are NTBs to intra-ASEAN trade. NTBs were supposed to be eliminated by 2010, except for the Philippines (by 2012) and CLMV (by 2015 with flexibility to 2018 for some products). It seems that many ASEAN countries are still struggling to remove NTBs. While Myanmar, Indonesia and the Philippines were countries applying most of the NTBs, Cambodia and Thailand were the least NTB-restrictive countries.

Rules of origin

AFTA started with a simple rules of origin (ROO) criterion of a 40 per cent regional value content (RVC), but, in response to business feedback, new options were introduced. These include using the change in tariff classification (CTC) and the product specific process rule; and abolition of the free-on-board (fob) value in the ASEAN Certificate of Origin Form D. A Pilot Sector Study on the most appropriate ROO to facilitate the integration of ASEAN production networks has been completed for automotive products and is working on other products such as iron and steel. The ROO have also been made more user-friendly with arrangements for back-to-back Certificate of Origin and third-party invoicing. Remaining issues with ROO include: arbitrary classification of origins resulting from differences in tariff classification among countries caused by slow adoption of the AHTN and the low utilisation of ASEAN tariff preferences. ASEAN is also involved in FTAs with China, South Korea, Japan, India and Australia–New Zealand, while individual ASEAN members have numerous bilateral FTAs. In all these, the multiple ROO regimes result in the ‘spaghetti-bowl effect’ that fragments production operations and raises business transaction costs.

5.4.2 *Trade facilitation measures*

Removal of tariffs and NTBs does not ensure free flow of goods among ASEAN countries and trade facilitation measures are also necessary. ASEAN is not a customs union and border procedures and inspections are necessary and pervasive (giving rise to corruption opportunities) and critically affect intra-ASEAN movement of goods. The ASEAN Trade Facilitation Framework and its Work Programme have been adopted to address issues such as integrating customs procedures, establishing the ASEAN Single Window, enhancing preferential tariff certification procedures, harmonising standards and conformance procedures. Problems with market access, border administration, transport and communications infrastructure incur additional trade costs.

Customs procedures

With the signing of the updated version of the ASEAN Agreement on Customs, the customs administrations are accelerating the necessary reforms and modernisation of customs techniques and procedures. The AHTN has been finalised, providing a single harmonised tariff classification. There is little apparent variation in countries' participation in formal ASEAN efforts to improve customs clearance procedures – still, only two countries have full electronic filing of customs documentation. The Strategic Plans of

Customs Development (SPCDs) for 2011–15 cover a wide range of activities. The adoption and the timely implementation of these SPCDs will reduce both processing cost and time required for the release of shipments. The SPCDs will also have a positive impact on the general customs administration and improve its efficiency in delivery.

Self-certification

This allows exporters to declare and self-certify the ASEAN product content in their exported products on pre-agreed export documents. ASEAN member states select eligible exporters as 'certified exporters' and empower them to make self-declaration on the agreed export documents. The first pilot project started in November 2010, with three participating countries (Brunei, Malaysia and Singapore) and was joined by Thailand in October 2011. Indonesia, Laos and the Philippines participated in the second pilot project in late 2012. On completion of the pilot project stage, participants of the two pilot projects will merge to have an ASEAN-wide implementation of the Self-Certification System by 2015. This will provide the business community with an added advantage in managing the cost and time of doing business in the region. The system will also allow for building trust through consultation and greater transparency between the business community and the public sector.

ASEAN Single Window

The ASEAN Single Window (ASW) programme aims to reduce transaction costs by speeding up clearance of shipments and release of goods by customs authorities. However, the programme has fallen behind schedule as it requires the prior establishment of national single windows (NSWs) by individual ASEAN countries. A fully operational NSW will allow traders to submit trade-related documents in one place and enable related agencies within a member state to process and deliver decisions through the same point where the submission was made. In some of the countries, businesses and industries are increasingly making use of the existing NSWs for submitting and processing customs declarations and fulfilling regulatory requirements. Currently, ASEAN countries are at various levels of development of their NSWs. The ASEAN6 countries still face challenges regarding their effectiveness – for example, Indonesia needs to improve coordination among offices involved in the NSW, human resource capacity in its customs office and related agencies, and new regulations made to implement the NSW; Thailand has a coordination problem among agencies involved in the NSW; the Philippines has problems of data standardisation and business process simplification. The CLMV had until 2012 to set up their NSWs but much more remains to be done. They will certainly require a huge effort to meet the 2015 AEC completion deadline. The ASW, when fully operational, will facilitate the movement of goods by providing the relevant architecture for the electronic exchange of cargo clearance documents among ASEAN states. A pilot project on ASW is being implemented with seven countries participating and the others joining in later.

Technical barriers, standards and conformance

ASEAN countries have national standards and technical regulations on domestically produced products as well as imported products for quality and public safety reasons. Sometimes they could be too strictly applied with a protectionist intent to impede the flow of imported goods. In 1992 ASEAN established the ASEAN Consultative Committee for Standards and Quality (ACCSQ) to reduce and, where possible, eliminate these technical barriers to trade. The ACCSQ focused on four main harmonising activities: national standards with international standards, practices and guides to eliminate conflict among national standards; mandatory technical requirements that include registration and pre-market approval requirements to ensure free movement of goods; conformity assessment procedures (accreditation, certification, testing and inspection, and mutual recognition of test reports and certification) to save transaction time and obviate the high cost of multiple testing; and technical regulations for national adoption. ASEAN also developed several sectoral MRAs, which are agreements made mutually to recognise or accept aspects of each other's assessments of product standards. Having an MRA would reduce the need for a product to undergo multiple tests in order to be sold or used in different ASEAN countries and thus reduce business costs on test reports and increase the certainty of market access for products. The ASEAN Framework Agreement on Mutual Recognition Agreements signed in 1998 has provided a framework for ASEAN member states to adopt MRAs for different sectors. MRAs have been concluded for the electrical and electronics sector and the pharmaceutical sector, while those for agro-based products and automotive sectors are ongoing. In 1997 work on harmonising standards began with the identification of twenty priority products; fifty-eight standards for electrical appliances and three standards for the rubber-based products sector were harmonised. ASEAN has harmonised the technical regulations for the cosmetics sector (under the ASEAN Harmonised Cosmetic Regulatory Scheme signed in 2003) and the electrical and electronics sector (under the ASEAN Harmonised Electrical and Electronics Equipment Regulatory Regime) signed in 2005. The harmonisation of technical regulations for other sectors is under way for agro-based products, automotive, medical devices, traditional medicine and health supplement sectors.

Trade logistics

Logistics encompass activities from transport, warehousing, cargo consolidation and border clearance to domestic distribution and payment systems. Logistics performance impacts on country competitiveness and export performance. Table 5.4 shows the World Bank Logistics Performance Index (LPI) for the ASEAN member states, except for Brunei. The LPI measures logistics efficiency – a country's ability to trade globally depends on its traders' access to global freight and logistics networks. The LPI's six components include: efficiency of customs and border management clearance; quality of trade and transport infrastructure; ease of arranging competitively priced shipments; competence and quality of logistics services; ability to track and trace consignments; and frequency with which shipments reach consignees within scheduled or expected delivery times. The 'logistics gap' among ASEAN member states is wide, with Singapore having the top rank out of 155 countries covered, while Myanmar ranks at the other end of the ASEAN spectrum.

Table 5.4 *ASEAN Logistics Performance Index, 2012*

	Logistics Performance Index rank	Logistics Performance Index score	Customs rank	Infrastructure rank	International shipping rank	Logistics quality rank	Tracking and tracing rank	Timelines rank
Brunei	n/a	n/a	n/a	n/a	n/a	n/a	n/a	n/a
Indonesia	59	2.94	75	85	57	62	52	42
Malaysia	29	3.49	29	27	26	30	28	28
Philippines	52	3.02	67	62	56	39	39	69
Singapore	1	4.13	1	2	2	6	6	1
Thailand	38	3.18	42	44	35	49	45	39
Cambodia	101	2.56	108	128	101	103	78	104
Laos	109	2.50	93	106	123	104	111	118
Myanmar	129	2.37	122	133	116	110	129	140
Vietnam	53	3.00	63	72	39	82	47	38

Source: World Bank, Connecting to Compete: Trade Logistics in the Global Economy (Washington, DC: World Bank, 2012).

Among the Index's components, Cambodia and Myanmar rank poorly on customs; Laos, Cambodia and Myanmar rank poorly for quality of infrastructure; Cambodia, Myanmar and Laos rank poorly on international shipping and on logistics quality; Laos and Myanmar on tracking and tracing of consignments; and Cambodia, Laos and Myanmar on timeliness of shipments in reaching destinations.

5.4.3 *Trade in services liberalisation*

The 'ASEAN minus X' formula was adopted in 2004 whereby negotiations are initiated when there is a minimum of three countries involved. Since the establishment of AFAS there have been five rounds of negotiations involving eight packages. These include a wide range of services sectors such as business and professional services, construction, distribution, education, environmental services, healthcare, maritime transport, telecommunications and tourism. Starting from the fifth package an AFAS package would comprise all commitments made by ASEAN states under the WTO, under earlier AFAS packages, and improved or new commitments made in the current package. Hence, stakeholders would have full information of the services commitment made by ASEAN states in both the WTO and AFAS by perusing the latest AFAS package. The eighth package is the most ambitious set of commitments to date. Subject to a limited pre-agreed flexibility, the commitments are in line with the targets set under the AEC Blueprint, which include: scheduling no restrictions for cross-border supply (Mode 1) and consumption abroad (Mode 2); allowing for foreign equity participation of 51 per cent or more (Mode 3); and progressively removing other restrictions. ASEAN states are expected to continue expanding the depth and breadth of their services commitments towards achieving free flow of services by 2015.

For each new group of sectors, the liberalisation commitments include:

- No restrictions on Mode 1 (cross-border trade), where neither producer nor consumer moves and trade often occurs via the internet, and Mode 2 (consumption abroad), where the consumer moves temporarily to the country of the producer. Exceptions are made for bona fide regulatory reasons such as public safety. With few exceptions, ASEAN countries have largely complied with this commitment, with construction the only problematic sector, where cross-border services remain unbound for many members.
- For Mode 3, there is no commitment to 100 per cent foreign (ASEAN) equity participation. Instead, the allowed foreign equity should be not less than 52 per cent by 2008, and 70 per cent by 2010 for the four priority sectors; not less than 49 per cent by 2008, 51 per cent by 2010 and 70 per cent by 2013 for logistics services; and not less than 49 per cent by 2008, 51 per cent by 2010 and 70 per cent by 2015 for other services sectors. For Mode 3, the parameters of liberalisation for national treatment limitations, and limitations in the horizontal commitments for each round are set by 2009 and schedule commitments

according to agreed parameters. All ASEAN countries (except Singapore) have fallen behind the liberalisation goals in terms of foreign equity participation. Domestic restrictions on equity and land holdings and licensing requirements continue to pose significant barriers to intra-regional investment in services. Since the AEC does not reach into behind-the-border issues, it is likely that these barriers will persist in the foreseeable future.

- For Mode 4, MRAs enable the qualifications of services suppliers recognised by the relevant authorities in their home country to be mutually recognised by other signatory ASEAN states. This promotes the flow of professional services providers in the ASEAN region in accordance with relevant domestic rules and regulations.

> Each member state may recognise the education or experience obtained, requirements met, or licences or certifications granted in another member state for the purpose of licensing or certification of service suppliers. Such recognition may be based upon an agreement or arrangement with the member state concerned or may be accorded autonomously.

MRAs have been concluded and signed on engineering services (2005); nursing services (2006); architectural services with a framework arrangement for the mutual recognition of surveying qualifications (2007); framework on accountancy services, on medical practitioners, and on dental practitioners (2009); and an MRA on tourism professionals was adopted in 2009. Various mechanisms are being established to administer the implementation of these MRAs. The

MRAs for engineers and architects provide a coordinating mechanism, while the MRAs for medical and dental practitioners focus on cooperation, with the aim of facilitating the recognition of qualified practitioners in other ASEAN states. The MRAs on accountancy and surveying services provide a framework of broad principles for further bilateral and multilateral negotiations among ASEAN states. Other MRAs for professional services are to be identified and negotiations completed by 2015.

Nikomborirak and Jitumrong (2013) argue that service liberalisation targets in the AEC are far from those required to support full integration.

- Concessions in AFAS are only marginally greater than those under GATS, except for Brunei, Indonesia, Myanmar and the Philippines.
- Liberalisation in Mode 3 envisions only a maximum of 70 per cent of ASEAN equity share. Liberalisation in Mode 4 is confined to movement of professionals, while unskilled labour is excluded. Even then, the MRA only provides an agreed framework to facilitate liberalisation, and there is no prescribed liberalisation obligation.
- The 'pre-agreed flexibilities to accommodate the interests of all ASEAN member states' cover subsectors totally excluded from liberalisation as well as subsectors in which not all the agreed parameters of liberalisation of the modes of supply are met. The scheduling of the liberalisation commitments in each round are accorded the following flexibilities – the possibility of catching up in the next round if a member is not able to meet the parameters of

commitments set for the previous round; allowing for substituting subsectors that have been agreed to be liberalised in a round, but for which a member is unable to make commitments, with subsectors outside the agreed subsectors; and liberalisation through the 'ASEAN minus X' formula. The flexibility provision is vague and seems to dilute what is supposed to be 'binding' commitments into nothing more than those based on 'best effort'.

5.4.4 Free flow of investment under AIA and ACIA

The ACIA superseded the AIA and took effect finally in March 2012. It attempts to offer an attractive FDI regime for ASEAN investors, providing national treatment and investor-state dispute resolution (including arbitration). It took three years after the signing of the ACIA in February 2009 to have it ratified, with delays in ratification by Thailand and Indonesia. ASEAN countries also delayed submitting their reservations lists even though they were required to submit within six months after its signing. The ACIA includes the earlier AIA provisions of investment liberalisation, investment facilitation and investment promotion as well as investment protection provisions formerly under a separate agreement in 1987. The ACIA adopts a negative list approach to the listing of reservations and provides for further liberalisation within set timelines in accordance with the AEC phases. It also contains new provisions on investor-state dispute settlement, transfers, treatment of investments, and new articles on prohibition of performance requirements. It aims to increase intra-ASEAN investments, especially by MNCs, and encourage expansion by SMEs.[8]

- *Investment liberalisation.* Free and open investment by 2015 with MFN and national treatment for investors (with limited exceptions); reduce/remove restrictions to entry for investments in the Priority Integration Sectors (PIS) covering goods; and reduce/remove restrictive investment measures and other impediments, including performance requirements. While all ASEAN countries welcome FDI, some countries (particularly Indonesia and Thailand) have long TELs and SLs on opening up to foreign investors and on according national treatment. ASEAN countries have started to consider amending regulatory regimes, if needed, to support changes in rules.
- *Investment facilitation.* More transparent, consistent and predictable investment rules, regulations, policies and procedures; harmonise, where possible, investment policies to achieve industrial complementation and economic integration; streamline and simplify procedures for investment applications and approvals; promote dissemination of investment information, rules, regulations, policies and procedures; strengthen databases on investment to facilitate policy formulation; strengthen coordination among the government ministries and agencies

[8] See Chia October 2013a.

concerned; and consult with ASEAN private sectors to facilitate investment and identify and work towards areas of complementation.

- *Investment promotion.* Promote ASEAN as an integrated investment area and production network; promote intra-ASEAN investments, especially from the ASEAN6 to CLMV; promote growth and development of SMEs as well as MNCs; promote industrial complementation and production networks among MNCs in ASEAN; promote joint investment missions that focus on regional clusters and production networks; and promote an effective network of bilateral agreements on avoidance of double taxation among ASEAN countries. ASEAN has intensified efforts through such initiatives as the linking of investment agencies' websites, development and dissemination of investment publications, and conduct of investment road shows and seminars.
- *Investment protection.* Provide enhanced protection to all investors and their investments; provisions on the investor-state dispute settlement mechanism; and transfer and repatriation of capital, profits, dividends etc.; provide transparent coverage of expropriation and compensation, full protection and security, and treatment of compensation for losses resulting from strife.

5.4.5 Freer flow of capital and financial integration

Financial integration in ASEAN will be accomplished through the following initiatives: financial services liberalisation, capital account liberalisation and capital market development.

Financial services liberalisation

Progressive liberalisation of financial services by 2015 aims to promote trade liberalisation by allowing greater access to financial services. Financial services liberalisation is addressed separately from AFAS. There are five packages of financial services commitments. Measures should allow members to ensure orderly development of the sector and maintenance of financial and socio-economic stability. The liberalisation target is extended to 2020 instead of 2015 and there is no prespecified scope of liberalisation in terms of both the breadth and depth of the commitment to be made. Member countries are allowed to carve out subsectors they do not wish to open up under the 'pre-agreed flexibilities', which limit the scope of liberalisation. In May 2011 ASEAN Finance Ministers concluded the fifth round of negotiations with the signing of the Protocol to Implement the Fifth Package of Commitments on Financial Services under AFAS. Subsequently, the sixth round of negotiations was launched to increase further business access to financial services. The Protocol to implement the Sixth Package of Commitments on Financial Services Liberalisation under AFAS was signed by ASEAN Finance Ministers in May 2014.

Capital market development

The construction of long-term infrastructures for developing ASEAN capital markets aims to promote cross-border collaboration among the various capital markets in the region. An 'Implementation Plan for an Integrated Capital Market' has been developed to enhance market access, linkages and liquidity. To address market gaps, a two-pronged approach to capital market development has been adopted. An action group was also established to engage dialogue among market experts to address existing obstacles to the creation of an integrated ASEAN bond market. Capacity building and technical assistance programmes for capital market development will be strengthened. An ASEAN Bond Market Development Scorecard was created to ensure the compliance of ASEAN capital markets with standards and a common framework in facilitating cross-border offerings and investment. On the ASEAN Capital Market Forum's (ACMF) initiatives, the significant progress that has been made since the fifteenth ASEAN Finance Ministers' Meeting (AFMM) includes: (1) the completion of the fully harmonised ASEAN Disclosure Standards, which is a set of common prospectus disclosure requirements to be adopted by ASEAN jurisdictions for cross-border primary offerings of securities; (2) the signing of the Memorandum of Understanding on the Expedited Review Framework for Secondary Listings by the stock exchanges and securities regulators of Malaysia, Singapore and Thailand to facilitate speedier processing of applications for secondary listings on participating stock exchanges; and (3) the launch of the ASEAN Corporate Governance Scorecard for assessing and ranking ASEAN publicly listed companies. Efforts to deepen equities markets were strengthened and the new working committees on dispute resolution and enforcement and taxation were established. The marketing and branding campaign for the ASEAN Exchanges initiative that promotes ASEAN as an asset class was launched in May 2011. In line with the development of local currency bond markets, the Credit Guarantee and Investment Facility (CGIF) was set up in October 2011, while the agreement for the US$400 million ASEAN Infrastructure Fund (AIF) was signed in September 2011 to mobilise funds for infrastructure financing in ASEAN.

Capital account liberalisation

The removal of capital controls and restrictions, including the elimination of restrictions on current account transactions, FDI, portfolio flows (inflows and outflows) and other types of flows, aims to facilitate the freer flow of capital in the ASEAN region. Substantial progress has been made in relaxing the limitations on foreign exchange purchases and other payments for invisible transactions and currency transfers. ASEAN states have completed the assessment and identification of rules for freer flows of FDI, portfolio investments and other types of flows and have started similar assessment exercises for restrictions on repatriation/surrender requirements. They have also begun to amend laws and regulations to promote FDI and portfolio investments.

East Asian financial stability and integration and surveillance and monitoring

ASEAN is pursuing a number of initiatives to support financial stability in East Asia and to encourage greater financial integration with China, Japan and South Korea.

The CMIM is a US$240 billion multilateral currency-swap facility launched in March 2010 and designed to assist countries with short-term liquidity difficulties. The ABMI, launched in 2005, aims to develop and deepen local currency bond markets in ASEAN+3 countries. Under the ABMI Roadmap, priorities focus on strengthening bond issuance, facilitating demand, enhancing regulatory regimes and building bond market infrastructure. The ASEAN Integration Monitoring Office (AIMO) was officially established in May 2010 to enhance the surveillance capacity of the ASEAN Secretariat to monitor regional economic integration, while at the same time ensuring the creation of the ASEAN Economic Community by 2015.

5.4.6 Free flow of skilled labour

Chia (March 2011) notes that factors driving skilled labour mobility in ASEAN include: large disparities in wages and employment opportunities; geographic proximity and socio-cultural-linguistic familiarity; and disparities in educational developments. As more ASEAN countries move up the technological ladder, liberalising trade in goods and services and in FDI would not be enough, and a larger pool of professional and skilled labour becomes necessary. Until such time when domestic educational and training institutions are able to supply the necessary high-level manpower, and domestic economic growth is able to absorb all the skilled manpower, ASEAN countries will still have to depend on importing or exporting talent.

Even with adequate domestic supply there is still a need for foreign talent, as it will provide the competition, stimulation and synergy to improve the quantity, quality and productivity of domestic talent. Some countries like Singapore and, to a lesser extent, Malaysia regard foreign talent as an upgrading and competitive tool and have policies to promote inflows of foreign professionals and skills. Most ASEAN countries, however, have yet to move away from constitutional provisions, policies, regulations and practices aimed at protecting domestic professionals and skilled workers from foreign competition.

Strategic actions on free flow of skilled labour in the AEC Blueprint include: facilitate issuance of visas and employment passes; MRAs for major professional services; core concordance of services skills and qualifications; and enhanced cooperation among ASEAN universities to increase regional mobility for students and staff. The ASEAN Agreement on Movement of Natural Persons was finalised in 2012, serving to facilitate the movement of persons engaged in trade and investment in ASEAN, establish streamlined and transparent procedures for temporary entry and stay as well as protect national borders and the domestic labour force.

Mutual Recognition Arrangements

The MRA is a major instrument for skilled labour mobility in ASEAN. Through MRAs, ASEAN countries may recognise the education or experience obtained, requirements met and licensing or certification granted by other ASEAN countries. However, as is clear from the

European experience, negotiating for recognition is a complex and time-consuming process given the wide differences in development levels and educational standards among ASEAN countries and the role of national professional associations. As discussed earlier under Mode 4 for services liberalisation, MRAs for professional qualifications have been completed in architecture, accountancy, surveying, engineering, for medical practitioners, dental practitioners and for nursing and tourism professionals, and other MRAs will be identified and negotiated by the 2015 deadline.

Chia (March 2011b) notes that effective implementation of these MRAs poses problems, as market access (permission to work) is subject to domestic rules and regulations. Policies and regulatory framework that constrain and impede skilled labour mobility include: requirements and procedures for employment visas and employment passes; constitutional provisions reserving jobs for nationals; policies that close or impose numerical caps on foreign professionals and skills in sectors and occupations; economic and labour market tests that constrain employment of foreigners and requiring them to be replaced by locals within a stipulated period; licensing regulations of professional associations; and language proficiency requirements. Countries should try to remove, as far as possible, impediments to free flow of skilled labour. More information exchange and transparency, and simplifying visa and employment-pass applications would help. National sensitivities to the migration issue have prevented much effective cooperation to date.

5.4.7 Priority integration sectors (PISs)

The twelve PISs identified are: agro-based goods, air transport, automotive products, electronics and electrical goods, fisheries, rubber-based goods, textiles and clothing, wood-based products, e-ASEAN, healthcare services, tourism and logistics services. New initiatives have been launched, including the development of the ASEAN Tourism Strategic Plan (2011–15), ASEAN Automotive Industry Strategy and MRAs for telecoms equipment. Most of the horizontal measures of the twelve PISs have been implemented, while the implementation of PIS-specific measures is still ongoing.

5.4.8 Food, agriculture and forestry

Food security remains a priority for ASEAN, with the establishment of the ASEAN Integrated Food Security (AIFS) Framework and its medium-term Strategic Plan of Action on ASEAN Food Security. Towards this end, reference diagnostic laboratories and phytosanitary guidelines for rice-milled products were implemented. Other measures focus on regulatory harmonisation of agricultural products to ensure free flow of safe and qualified products and to improve competitiveness in international markets, as well as the development of national good agricultural practices. ASEAN has also pursued new cooperation initiatives with external partners under the ASEAN+3 process to promote food security, including the ASEAN Plus Three Emergency Rice Reserve (APTERR) Agreement, and the APT

Comprehensive Strategy on Food Security and Bio-energy Development (APTCS-FSBD).

5.4.9 *Realising a competitive economic region*

This pillar has several behind-the-border actions to reinforce ASEAN competitiveness in addition to border liberalisation measures on goods, services, investment and capital and labour movements (see the AEC Blueprint 2008).

Competition policy

Several initiatives for competition policy were set up, including the formation of the ASEAN Experts Group on Competition. The ASEAN Regional Guidelines on Competition Policy and the Handbook on Competition Policy and Laws in ASEAN for Business were launched to promote healthy competition and fair business practices. The Guidelines provide a good reference on country experiences and best practices at the international level, while the Handbook provides basic notions of substantive and procedural competition law applicable in ASEAN countries.

Consumer protection

With the mandate of the newly established ASEAN Committee on Consumer Protection (ACCP), ASEAN endorsed the Guidelines for Notification and Information Exchange on Recalled/Banned Products in October 2011. Initial work was undertaken to develop the 'cross-border redress website' that would serve as the main reference point for matters pertaining to consumer redress. Dissemination of the ASEAN Consumer

Complaints leaflet is also under way to increase awareness of visitors/tourists on the rights of consumers in ASEAN.

Intellectual property rights

The role of IPR divides the producers (who are mainly developed countries) and the developing country users. The ASEAN countries' position is primarily that of developing country users, although Singapore has significant interest in IPR protection while other ASEAN countries are more concerned with protection of their traditional and indigenous cultures, medicines and plants. Development of intellectual property and IPR is crucial to building an innovative and competitive economic region. As such, ASEAN has strengthened intellectual property institutions and carried out new initiatives. In August 2011 the ASEAN IPR Action Plan 2011–15 was endorsed. ASEAN also collaborated with Dialogue Partners and international organisations to enhance capacity building of ASEAN countries in the area of intellectual property. Conflicts of interest among ASEAN countries are rare[9] and the main conflicts are enforcing the IPR of developed countries and foreign MNCs in regard to manufactured branded products, patented medicines, computer software and online music and movies.

Infrastructure development

Transportation (land, air, sea) and information technology (IT) infrastructure are essential for the movement of goods,

[9] There have been recent spats, particularly between Indonesia and Malaysia, over the origins and IPR of some songs and cuisines.

capital, labour, people and ideas among and between ASEAN countries. The Brunei Action Plan adopted in 2010 contains strategic actions to be implemented in 2011–15 towards the realisation of AEC as well as new priorities under the Master Plan on ASEAN Connectivity.

- The signing of the ASEAN Multilateral Agreement on the Full Liberalisation of Passenger Air Services and its protocol provided a framework for full realisation of ASEAN Open Skies.
- To facilitate ASEAN shipping services by reducing substantial restrictions to ASEAN shipping services, the Strategy Toward the Integration of ASEAN Single Shipping Market (ASSM) was developed to serve as basic reference to developing ASSM in the future.
- ASEAN also completed the stocktaking of road inventory of all national route components of the ASEAN Highway Network to strengthen the ASEAN regional infrastructure.
- The ASEAN ICT Masterplan 2015 was adopted in January 2011 to set a common direction and actions in driving and stimulating the right ICT development in the region. Among the key initiatives are the ASEAN Broadband Corridor and the ASEAN Internet Exchange.
- ASEAN completed the study on Adoption of ASEAN Technical Architecture Framework for e-commerce interoperability.
- ASEAN energy cooperation, driven by the ASEAN Plan of Action on Energy Cooperation (APAEC) 2010–15, consists of seven key programme areas of cooperation that aim to

enhance energy security, accessibility and sustainability for ASEAN: ASEAN Power Grid, Trans-ASEAN Gas Pipeline, Coal and Clean Technology, Renewable Energy, Energy Efficiency and Conservation, Regional Energy Policy and Planning and Civilian Nuclear Energy.

- With regard to infrastructure development in ASEAN, the necessary domestic legislation has yet to be enacted for the ASEAN Framework Agreement on Multilateral Transport, the ASEAN Framework Agreement on Inter-State Transport, the ASEAN Multilateral Agreement on Full Liberalisation of Passenger Air Services, Protocol 6 of the ASEAN Framework Agreement on the Facilitation of Goods in Transit (AFAFGIT), the ASEAN Single Shipping Market, and the ASEAN Interconnection Projects. In 2010 the Master Plan on ASEAN Connectivity was adopted, with an estimated US$60 billion annual infrastructure investment needed for the 2010–20 period. The ASEAN Infrastructure Fund commenced operation in May 2012.

A major challenge in ASEAN infrastructure development is coordinating the various national needs with the regional vision and plans to avoid costly overlaps and ensure no missing links. National needs often take precedence because governments have to fulfil demands of their own constituencies. An important element for developing a regional infrastructure network is the harmonisation of various national infrastructure standards so as to facilitate the flows of goods and people. Issues and challenges in ASEAN infrastructure development include the need for: an effective regional institutional mechanism to implement infrastructure cooperation and projects; the establishment of a planning mechanism that can coordinate and streamline national and regional infrastructure planning and needs; and effective monitoring of the implementation of infrastructure projects. As infrastructure financing needs are huge, ASEAN needs to explore various funding mechanisms and sources. As noted earlier, an ASEAN Infrastructure Fund has been established.

5.4.10 Realising equitable economic development

The AEC Blueprint only lists two measures in this area, namely, SME development targeted to narrow intra-country development gaps and the IAI targeted at narrowing the development gap between ASEAN6 and CLMV.

Development of SMEs

This is necessary to mitigate market dominance by foreign MNCs and large state-owned enterprises (SOEs), thus fostering local entrepreneurship and innovation, employment creation and a more equitable development model. SMEs in ASEAN face several challenges, including limited access to finance and technology, severe competition from MNCs and SMEs of other countries such as China, Japan and Korea, weak entrepreneurial and management skills, lack of awareness of AEC initiatives and benefits, and difficulties in coping with AEC preferences and market standards.

To enhance the competitiveness and resilience of SMEs, the Strategic Action Plan for the ASEAN SME Development (2010–15) was endorsed in August 2010 to give guidance on the various SME initiatives: the ASEAN SME Advisory Board provides strategic policy inputs on SME development to the Ministers and guidance on high-priority matters to the ASEAN SME Working Group; ASEAN started to work on the development of the Conceptual Framework for Regional SME Development Fund; two projects under the Strategic Action Plan have been completed, namely, the ASEAN Multi-media Self-reliant System Toolkit Package and the Feasibility Study of the SME Service Centre; and the Directory of Outstanding ASEAN SMEs 2011 seeks to promote linkages of SMEs to the regional and global supply chains and production networks.

Initiative for ASEAN Integration

Initiative for ASEAN Integration (IAI) serves as a platform for identifying and implementing technical assistance and capacity building programmes largely targeted at CLMV. The new IAI Strategic Framework and Work Plans I and II were endorsed to facilitate the implementation of CLMV projects. The scope of priority areas has been expanded beyond infrastructure, human resource development, ICT and capacity building for regional integration to also cover tourism, poverty and quality of life. The ASEAN6, ASEAN Dialogue Partners and the ADB are involved in the IAI programmes. The nineteenth ASEAN Summit in November 2011 endorsed the ASEAN Framework on Equitable Economic Development (EED) as a new initiative.

Vo Tri (2013) analysed the effectiveness of the IAI based on survey responses and came to the following conclusions.

- Overall, CLMV countries have a positive perception of the IAI programmes and projects, as they embody significant relevance to the development needs and priorities of CLMV. Still, there are some problems. Better outcomes would have been realised if the design and implementation of IAI work plans achieved better financial adequacy through donor coordination. On whether IAI programme areas/projects contribute to narrowing development gaps, the survey responses found that such contribution has been either moderate or substantial. On the relevance of IAI work plans to the needs and development priorities of CLMV, the majority of survey responses expressed an appreciation of these initiatives.
- Notwithstanding the positive responses from the survey, Vo Tri argues that specific IAI programme areas may not fully fit with key priorities of individual CLMV countries and that there is danger in using a common template for CLMV countries. Further, even if the areas and projects under the IAI are appropriate, they may be too ambitious given the financial resources and time constraints and would call for better coordination of programmes by donors, including the World Bank and the ADB. Additionally, the IAI may not pay enough attention to institution building. For example, Singapore could take the lead in supporting and cooperating with CLMV in finance, ICT, healthcare, education, urban development, institution building and logistics, while Thailand could guide CLMV in promoting tourism, agricultural development and macroeconomic management.

5.4.11 *External economic relations*

Of the four pillars of the AEC, the best performance in implementation is in the measures and actions to integrate ASEAN into the global economy. ASEAN has successfully negotiated FTAs with China, Japan, South Korea, India and Australia-New Zealand.

ASEAN–China free trade agreement

The Framework Agreement on Comprehensive Economic Cooperation between ASEAN and China was signed in 2002, providing the framework for ASEAN and China to negotiate further agreements leading to the creation of the ASEAN–China free trade agreement (ACFTA). China has since become ASEAN's largest trading partner, with trade reaching US$280.4 billion in 2011 to account for 11.7 per cent of ASEAN's total trade. ACFTA had a market size of 1.94 billion consumers and a combined GDP of US$9.5 trillion in 2011. The Agreement on Trade in Goods was signed in 2004 with tariff reduction and elimination under the 'normal track' and 'sensitive track'. Tariffs in the normal track are to be eliminated by ASEAN6 and China by January 2012, and by CLMV by January 2015, with flexibility to eliminate tariffs on products not exceeding 250 tariff lines by January 2018. There is no exclusion of products allowed. The ROO follow a general rule of RVC at 40 per cent, with 527 tariff lines at a six-digit level subject to product-specific rules. The ROO are being reviewed to make them more liberal and encourage business utilisation of ACFTA. The Agreement on Trade in Services was signed in January 2007. The Protocol to Implement the

Second Package of Commitments went into effect in January 2012. The Investment Agreement was signed in August 2009. It stipulates key protection elements for ensuring fair and equitable treatment for investors, non-discriminatory treatment on nationalisation or expropriation and compensation for losses. It also has provisions allowing for transfers and repatriation of profits in a freely usable currency and provides investors recourse to arbitration to settle investor-state disputes.

ASEAN–Japan Comprehensive Economic Partnership

The ASEAN–Japan Comprehensive Economic Partnership (AJCEP) was signed in April 2008 and covers trade in goods, trade in services, investment and economic cooperation. As of 2011, ASEAN and Japan had a combined GDP of US$8 trillion, and total bilateral trade of US$273.3 billion. Japan must eliminate 92 per cent of its tariff rates while ASEAN6 and Vietnam must eliminate 90 per cent of their tariff rates in the Normal Track of the FTA within ten years of the Agreement's entry into force, while CLM must eliminate 90 per cent of tariff rates in the Normal Track within thirteen years. For goods under the HSL, SL and Exclusion List the modality varies and the tariff cuts were negotiated bilaterally between ASEAN states and Japan. ROO are aimed at encouraging regional cumulation of inputs that benefit both ASEAN industries and Japanese companies operating in ASEAN, with a 'general rule' of RVC 40 per cent or change in tariff heading (CTH) that allows exporters and manufacturers to choose which rule to apply under the Agreement. The Trade in Services

Agreement and the Investment Agreement are under negotiation and were targeted for completion in 2013 but not yet finalised as of end – 2014.

ASEAN–Korea Free Trade Area

In 2005 ASEAN and Korea signed the Framework Agreement on Comprehensive Economic Cooperation, leading to agreements establishing the ASEAN–Korea Free Trade Area (AKFTA). The Trade in Goods Agreement was signed in 2006, involving tariff reduction and elimination for all tariff lines over a transition period. On 1 January 2012 Korea and ASEAN5 (Brunei, Indonesia, Malaysia, the Philippines and Singapore) eliminated tariffs on all products in the Normal Track, while CLMV were granted a longer transition period – for Vietnam, at least 50 per cent of tariff lines under the Normal Track will enjoy a 0 per cent to 5 per cent tariff rate by January 2013, and for CLM by January 2015. By 2017 and 2020 products under Vietnam and CLM's Normal Track would have zero tariffs. Thailand has a different schedule, with tariffs in the Normal Track reduced over a transition period and eliminated by either 2016 or 2017. The Trade in Services Agreement was signed in 2007. Building on their existing commitments in the GATS, ASEAN and Korea both increased their commitments through the addition of new sectors/sub-sectors, easing restrictions on a wide range of service sectors including business, construction, education, communication services, the environment, tourism services and transport services. The Agreement on Investment was signed in 2009. It includes provisions for fair and equitable treatment and full protection and security of covered investments; transfers of funds relating to covered investments; and compensation in the event of nationalisation or expropriation. ASEAN and Korea will hold discussions on investment agenda items and plan to conclude discussions within five years from the agreement's entry into force. The Agreement on Dispute Settlement Mechanism was signed in 2005.

ASEAN–India Free Trade Area

The ASEAN–India Free Trade Area (AIFTA) Trade in Goods Agreement was signed in 2009, covering a market of 1.8 billion people with a combined GDP of US$3.84 trillion and bilateral trade of US$68.4 billion in 2011. It provides for progressive tariff reduction and/or elimination. Under the Normal Track, tariffs imposed by ASEAN5 (that is, excluding the Philippines) and India will be eliminated by 2016, those between the Philippines and India by 2019 and an even longer time frame for CLMV. Under the Sensitive Track, goods with applied MFN rates of above 5 per cent will be reduced to 5 per cent for ASEAN5 and India by 2016, for the Philippines and India by 2019, and for CLMV by 2021. It also provides for different tariff rates for special products, such as crude and refined palm oil, coffee, black tea and pepper. There are also goods placed under the highly sensitive lists and exclusion lists, subject to an annual review. A general ROO of RVC 35 per cent plus change in tariff sub-heading (CTSH) is applied while product-specific rules are being negotiated to provide alternative rules for certain products and sectors. Negotiations on services and investment agreements were finalised in October 2013.

ASEAN–Australia–New Zealand Free Trade Area

The ASEAN–Australia–New Zealand Free Trade Area (AANZFTA) agreement was signed in 2009 to integrate twelve markets with 632 million people, a combined GDP of US$3.82 trillion and a trade value of US$67.7 billion in 2011. The agreement covers trade in goods and services and investment. On trade in goods, it was agreed progressively to liberalise tariffs and to eliminate tariffs on at least 90 per cent of all tariff lines. It was also agreed to facilitate the movement of goods by implementing specific provisions on ROO, customs procedures, sanitary and phytosanitary measures and standards, technical regulations and conformity assessment procedures. On trade in services, it was agreed to liberalise barriers and allow for greater market access for services suppliers. The agreement also provides for the free movement of people engaged in trade and investment activities and provides protection for investments, including compensation for losses, transfers relating to profit and capital and transfer of rights or claims to investments.

5.5 What the AEC Scorecard tells

While the AEC Blueprint provides a road map with strategic schedules for implementation, the AEC Scorecard (2012)[10] tracks the implementation, gaps and challenges of the various measures and strategic schedules in the Blueprint. The Scorecard only records compliance/non-compliance with

[10] ASEAN Secretariat 2012b.

the measures and gives no indication whether these measures and their implementation are adequate to achieve the AEC declared objectives by 2015.

5.5.1 *What has been implemented?*

Table 5.5 details the Scorecard for Phase I (2008–9) and Phase II (2010–11), showing implementation of measures for the AEC's four pillars and their components. Regrettably, the compliance/performance of individual ASEAN members are not made public. There do not appear to be penalties for defaulters.

Highlights of the Scorecard are as follows.

- For 2008–11, the implementation rates are 65.9 per cent for the single market and production base, 67.9 per cent for competitive economic region, 66.7 per cent for equitable economic development and 85.7 per cent for integration into the global economy. The implementation rates are higher for the earlier period than for the later period; thus, instead of accelerating implementation, ASEAN countries seem to be slowing down. This is a worrisome trend on two counts: first, the deadline of 2015 to complete the AEC is drawing very close; second, it would not be unreasonable to assume that the earlier successes are those that could be more easily implemented while remaining commitments would be more difficult to implement.
- For the single market and production base, in Phase I only four out of sixty-five measures were not fully implemented, and these were in free flow of services (3) and free flow of

Table 5.5 *AEC Scorecard*

	Phase I (2008–9)		Phase II (2010–11)		Total measures	
Key areas	Fully implemented	Not fully implemented	Fully implemented	Not fully implemented	Fully implemented	Not fully implemented
Single market and production base						
Free flow of goods	9	0	23	24	32	24
Free flow of services	10	3	13	17	23	20
Free flow of investment	5	1	5	8	10	9
Freer flow of capital	1	0	5	0	6	0
Free flow of skilled labour	–	–	1	0	1	0
Priority integration sectors	28	0	1	0	29	0
Food, agriculture and forestry	8	0	5	6	13	6
Total number of measures	61	4	53	55	114	59
Implementation rate (%)	93.8		49.1		65.9	

Competitive economic region						
Competition policy	2	0	2	0	4	0
Consumer protection	2	0	5	4	7	4
Intellectual property rights	–	–	4	1	4	1
Transport	15	10	6	8	21	18
Energy	0	0	2	1	2	1
Mineral	1	0	7	0	8	0
ICT	2	0	4	0	6	0
Taxation	–	–	0	1	0	1
e-commerce	–	–	1	0	1	0
Total number of measures	22	10	31	15	53	25
Implementation rate (%)	68.7		67.4		67.9	
Equitable economic development						
SME development	1	0	4	3	5	3
IAI	2	0	1	1	3	1

Table 5.5 (*cont.*)

Key areas	Phase I (2008–9)		Phase II (2010–11)		Total measures	
	Fully implemented	Not fully implemented	Fully implemented	Not fully implemented	Fully implemented	Not fully implemented
Total number of measures	3	0	5	4	8	4
Implementation rate (%)	100		55.5		66.7	
Integration into global economy						
External economic relations	5	0	7	2	12	2
Total number of measures	5	0	7	2	12	2
Implementation rate (%)	100		78		85.7	

Source: ASEAN Secretariat, *ASEAN Economic Community Scorecard: Charting Progress Towards Regional Economic Integration* (Jakarta: ASEAN Secretariat, 2012).

investment. For Phase II, fifty-five out of 108 measures were not fully implemented, and these were in free flow of goods (24), free flow of services (17), free flow of investment (8) and food agriculture and forestry (6). Thus the highest non-implementation rate for 2008–11 is in free flow of services, followed by free flow of investment. The main problem with services implementation is discussed later. The key problem with investments implementation is enforceability, as temporary exclusion and sensitive lists allow ASEAN countries to delay or opt out of implementing measures. Two outstanding measures requiring further action for investment liberalisation are: first, all measures under the AIA temporary exclusion list (TEL) and sensitive list (SL) under ACIA need to be subsumed upon entry into force of the ACIA; second, activities on investment promotion and facilitation need to be conducted as scheduled.

- For the competitive economic region, in Phase I, some ten out of thirty-two measures are not fully implemented, and these are primarily in transport. For Phase II, fifteen out of forty-six measures are not fully implemented and these are in transport (8), consumer protection (4), intellectual property rights, energy and taxation (1 each). Shortfalls in implementation on transport are mainly owing to delays in ratification of regional agreements and translating them into respective national laws. Most of these regional agreements are signed after years of consultation.
- For equitable economic development and integration into the global economy, non-full implementations are found only in Phase II.

5.5.2 *Deficiencies in the Scorecard Report*

The Scorecard Report is supposed to provide all information about the progress in the implementation of the AEC Blueprint, that is, whether the measures listed have been fully implemented as scheduled or whether there have been deficiencies in implementation and the reasons therefor. But this is not the case. According to the Scorecard, during the period under consideration, there were forty-seven measures associated with free flow of goods that have to be implemented, but only twenty-three have been fully implemented, and the remaining twenty-four are yet to be fully implemented. The Scorecard Report in its current form is not very useful for private-sector use and for independent scholarly analysis.

- The aggregate scores fail to reveal the true rates of implementation for individual countries and for different parts of a country (for example, the capital city versus other provinces and regions) and on each of the policy actions in the Blueprint, except as given in Table 5.6 below. By not making public the compliance record of individual countries, there is no 'public' pressure for compliance, particularly when there is no penalty for non-compliance.
- The Scorecard does not provide information on the reason/reasons for failures fully to implement specific measures. It gives no indication on the difficulties in implementation faced by each ASEAN country and what possible remedial actions could be taken. For example, no explanations were offered on why ASEAN took more than two years to ratify

Table 5.6 *Implementation of AEC Scorecard by country*

	Brunei	Cambodia	Indonesia	Laos	Malaysia	Myanmar	Philippines	Singapore	Thailand	Vietnam	ASEAN
Phase I (2008–9)											
Free flow of goods	A	A	A	A	A	A	A	A	A	A	A
Free flow of services	B	B	B	B	B	B	B	B	B	B	B
Free flow of investment	A	A	A	A	A	A	A	A	A	A	A
Freer flow of capital	A	A	A	A	A	A	A	A	A	A	A
Priority integration sectors	A	A	A	A	A	A	A	A	A	A	A
Food, agriculture, forestry	A	A	A	A	A	A	A	A	A	A	A
Competition policy	A	A	A	A	A	A	A	A	A	A	A
Consumer protection	A	A	A	A	A	A	A	A	A	A	A
Transport	B	B	B	B	B	B	B	B	B	B	B
Mineral	A	A	A	A	A	A	A	A	A	A	A

Table 5.6 (*cont.*)

	Brunei	Cambodia	Indonesia	Laos	Malaysia	Myanmar	Philippines	Singapore	Thailand	Vietnam	ASEAN
Information and communication technology	A	A	A	A	A	A	A	A	A	A	A
SME development	A	A	A	A	A	A	A	A	A	A	A
Initiative for ASEAN Integration	A	A	A	A	A	A	A	A	A	A	A
External economic relations	A	A	A	A	A	A	A	A	A	A	A
Phase II (2010–11)											
Free flow of goods	B	B	B	B	B	B	B	B	B	B	C
Free flow of services	B	B	B	B	B	B	B	B	B	B	C
Free flow of investment	B	B	B	B	B	B	B	B	C	B	C
Freer flow of capital	A	A	A	A	A	B	A	A	A	A	A
Free flow of skilled labour	A	A	A	A	A	A	A	A	A	A	A

Priority integration sectors	A	A	A	A	A	A	A	A	A	A	A
Food, agriculture, forestry	C	C	C	C	C	C	C	C	C	C	C
Competition policy	A	A	A	A	A	A	A	A	A	A	A
Consumer protection	B	B	B	B	B	B	B	B	B	B	B
Intellectual property rights	B	B	A	B	A	B	A	A	A	A	B
Transport	B	B	C	B	B	B	B	B	B	B	C
Energy	B	B	B	B	B	B	B	B	B	B	B
Mineral	A	A	A	A	A	A	A	A	A	A	A
Information and communication technology	A	A	A	A	A	A	A	A	A	A	A
Taxation	A	C	A	A	A	A	A	A	A	A	C
e-commerce	A	A	A	A	A	A	A	A	A	A	A
SME development	B	B	A	B	A	B	B	A	A	B	B
IAI	B	B	B	B	B	B	B	B	B	B	B

Table 5.6 (*cont.*)

	Brunei	Cambodia	Indonesia	Laos	Malaysia	Myanmar	Philippines	Singapore	Thailand	Vietnam	ASEAN
External economic relations	B	B	B	B	B	B	B	B	B	B	B
Phases I and II											
Free flow of goods	B	B	B	B	B	B	B	B	B	B	B
Free flow of services	B	B	B	B	B	B	B	B	B	B	B
Free flow of investment	B	B	B	B	B	B	B	B	B	B	B
Freer flow of capital	A	A	A	A	A	B	A	A	A	A	A
Free flow of skilled labour	A	A	A	A	A	A	A	A	A	A	A
Priority integration sectors	A	A	A	A	A	A	A	A	A	A	A
Food, agriculture, forestry	B	B	B	B	B	B	B	B	B	B	B
Competition policy	A	A	A	A	A	A	A	A	A	A	A
Consumer protection	B	B	B	B	B	B	B	B	B	B	B

Intellectual property rights	B	B	A	B	A	B	A	A	A	A	B
Transport	B	B	B	B	B	B	B	B	B	B	B
Energy	B	B	B	B	B	B	B	B	B	B	B
Mineral	A	A	A	A	A	A	A	A	A	A	A
Information and communication technology	A	A	A	A	A	A	A	A	A	A	A
Taxation	A	C	A	A	A	A	A	A	A	A	C
e-commerce	A	A	A	A	A	A	A	A	A	A	A
SME development	B	B	A	B	A	B	B	A	A	B	B
Initiative for ASEAN Integration	B	B	B	B	B	B	B	B	B	B	B
External economic relations	B	B	B	B	B	B	B	B	B	B	B

A = all measures targeted in this area were implemented; B = more than half of measures indicated in this area were implemented; C = less than half of measures indicated in this area were implemented.

Source: ASEAN Secretariat, *ASEAN Economic Community Scorecard: Charting Progress Towards Regional Economic Integration* (Jakarta: ASEAN Secretariat, 2012).

the ACIA, which is expected to enhance investment inflows and should be viewed as a positive-sum game.

- What does 'fully implemented' mean? The Scorecard Report explains that 'failure of one country to move and implement the measures may result in non-implementation of regional measures'. Effective implementation entails translating regional initiatives into domestic laws, strengthening internal coordination mechanisms among member states and actual use of the initiatives and measures by ASEAN businesses. For example, how is an MRA for medical practitioners implemented when entry and establishment are subject to domestic laws and regulations such as visa requirements, employment permit requirements, language requirements and constitutional provisions barring employment of foreign professionals?
- The Scorecard only reports compliance/non-compliance by governments in implementing the specific actions and measures indicated in the AEC Blueprint. It gives no indication of how far the objectives of the AEC regarding the single market and production base, a competitive economic region, equitable economic development and integration into the global economy are being realised. In other words, are the measures and actions taken adequate to realise the AEC?

Table 5.6 above shows the implementation record of individual ASEAN countries according to whether all targeted measures were implemented, more than half implemented or less than half implemented for the nineteen areas listed.

The highlights are:

- All ASEAN countries fully implemented freer flow of capital (except Myanmar), free flow of skilled labour and priority integration sectors, competition policy, mineral, ICT, taxation (except Cambodia) and e-commerce.
- All ASEAN countries more than half implemented free flow of goods, free flow of services, free flow of investments, food-agriculture-forestry, consumer protection, transport, energy, IAI and external economic relations.
- The compliance record is mixed, with full implementation in IPR for Malaysia, the Philippines, Singapore, Thailand and Vietnam, and more than half implementation in Brunei, Cambodia, Laos and Myanmar; and in SME development with full implementation in Indonesia, Malaysia, Singapore and Thailand, and more than half implementation in the other ASEAN countries.

5.5.3 *Implementing the AEC Blueprint by 2015*

Realisation of the AEC could mean full implementation of all the actions and measures listed in the AEC Blueprint or realising the AEC objectives of a single market and production base, a competitive economic region, equitable economic development and integration into the global economy. The first would be easier to achieve, while the second would require measures beyond those set out in the AEC Blueprint.

The immediate priority is to improve the implementation of the AEC Blueprint's strategic actions so that the 2015 timelines can be met. Problematic areas in the 2008–11 implemented period as set out in Table 5.7 are measures pertaining to services liberalisation, trade facilitation and free flow of skilled labour.

- It is crucial that efforts are intensified at both regional and country levels to close the implementation gaps. This calls for political will by ASEAN states to implement commitments. The ability to ratify economic agreements without prolonged delay is an important issue. There is a need to address the legislative and regulatory limitations that impede implementation. Also, countries need to strengthen their respective national coordinating agencies effectively to coordinate implementation across various ministries and agencies.
- The lack of political will to implement commitments is often due to the difficulties of convincing legislators, business enterprises and the general public of the benefits of trade and investment liberalisation. In any FTA, there are winners and losers. Winners are businesses, workers, investors and consumers that gain directly from liberalisation. Losers are those businesses and workers that face intensified competition from foreign imports and foreign investors. Policy makers have the tough task of marketing the liberalisation idea, seeking consultations with the private sector and workers to identify short-term losers, and finding mechanisms to 'compensate' losers through financial, technical and job training assistance to enable firms to seek new businesses and workers to find new jobs. Some ASEAN countries have been more successful than others in achieving this objective.

Table 5.7 *Outstanding measures under Phase I (2008–9) and Phase II (2010–11)*

	Measures to be implemented	Actions required
Phase I (2008–9)		
1	Completion of seventh package of trade in services liberalisation commitments	Schedule PIS sectors that meet the required higher foreign equity participation levels in subsequent AFAS packages
2	Entry into force of the ACIA	Endorse the ACIA Reservation Lists
3	Entry into force of the Protocols 1, 2, 7 and 9 of ASEAN Framework Agreement on the Facilitation of Goods in Transit (AFAFGIT)	Finalise and ratify protocols
4	Entry into force of the Agreement and Protocols 1 and 2 of the ASEAN Multilateral Agreement on the Full Liberalisation of Air Freight Services (MAAFS)	Expedite ratification of the agreement and its protocols.
Phase II (2010–11)		
1	Trade facilitation	Conduct scheduled study and assessment related with implementation of ROO and country assessment on trade facilitation
2	Customs facilitation and integration	Modernise tariff classification, customs valuation and customs techniques (that is, implement ASEAN Cargo Processing Model, ASEAN Customs Declaration Documents, Pre-arrival Clearance for customs clearance and cargo release) Establish ASEAN Customs Transit System Promote mutual assistance in customs Implement measures under ASEAN Single Window

Table 5.7 (*cont.*)

	Measures to be implemented	Actions required
3	Standards and conformance	Finalise MRA for Prepared Foodstuff and Automotive Finalise ASEAN Medical Device Directive Agreement Endorse ASEAN Regulatory Framework on Traditional Medicines and Health Supplement and transpose into national legislation Harmonise ASEAN Harmonised Electricity and Electronic Equipment Regulatory Regime to the listed standards and complete agreed conformity assessment procedures for regulated EEE
4	Services liberalisation	Finalise commitments under 8th Package and schedule the sectors to be liberalised up to 2012 Expedite ratification of the 5th Package of Commitments on Financial Services Finalise negotiation of Movement of Natural Persons (MNP) Agreement
5	Investment liberalisation, promotion and facilitation	Subsume all measures under AIA Temporary Exclusion Lists and Sensitive Lists under ACIA upon entry into force of the ACIA Conduct activities in support of investment promotion and facilitation as scheduled

6	Food, agriculture and forestry	Harmonise Quarantine and Inspection procedures
		Align the National GAP programme with ASEAN GAP
		Develop Guidelines on Compartmentalisation of Livestock Production
7	Consumer protection	Develop a comprehensive website on the ASEAN Cross-Border Consumer Redress
8	Infrastructure development	Enact the necessary domestic legislation to effect the ASEAN Framework Agreement on Multi-Modal Transport
		Conclude Protocol 6 (railway borders and interchange stations) under ASEAN Framework Agreement on Facilitation of Goods in Transit
		Ratify the ASEAN Framework Agreement on Inter-state Transport
		Ratify the ASEAN Multilateral Agreement on Full Liberalisation of Passenger Air Services
		Complete the activities scheduled under ASEAN Single Shipping Market
		Implement the ASEAN Interconnection Projects

Table 5.7 (*cont.*)

	Measures to be implemented	Actions required
9	Taxation	Complete the Network of Bilateral Agreements on Avoidance of Double Taxation among all AMSs
10	SME development	Implement the common Curriculum for Entrepreneurship in all ASEAN member states
		Establish a comprehensive SME Service Centre at national level
11	Initiative for ASEAN Integration	Complete the list of proposed activities under IAI
12	Development of FTAs	Finalise ASEAN–India services and investment negotiations
		Implement the ASEAN–Japan Comprehensive Economic Partnership by all member states

Source: ASEAN Secretariat, *ASEAN Economic Community Scorecard: Charting Progress Towards Regional Economic Integration* (Jakarta: ASEAN Secretariat, 2012).

- Monitoring of the progress of the AEC should be strengthened. There is a need to improve the monitoring capacity of the ASEAN Secretariat and provide technical assistance to member states to enhance their implementation capacity. Greater private-sector feedback should be solicited to assess the impact and effectiveness of the policies and measures being implemented, so as to address the impediments that prevent the free flow of goods, services, investments and capital.

5.6 Economic integration outcome indicators

While the Scorecard above measures implementation of AEC Blueprint measures, in March 2013 the ASEAN Secretariat released a report providing outcome indicators of ASEAN's progress towards the AEC (and ASCC). These outcome indicators for the AEC are summarised in Table 5.8 below.

5.6.1 Towards a single market and production base

- Trade in goods liberalisation. Intra-ASEAN trade in goods has been growing stronger, particularly from 2009 as the impact of the global financial crisis started to recede. The intra-ASEAN trade share rose marginally from 24.3 per cent in 2004 to 25 per cent in 2011.
- Price convergence. Overall price variance in terms of a broad basket of products declined, reflecting more integrated ASEAN markets.

Table 5.8 *Progress towards the AEC: selected indicators*

Outcome Indicators	Benchmark year	Benchmark value	Latest year	Latest value	Status
Goods trade liberalisation, and single market and production base					
Total trade in goods					
Intra-ASEAN total (US$ billion)	2004	260.9	2011	598.2	increasing
Intra-ASEAN share (%)	2004	24.3	2011	25.0	increasing
Extra-ASEAN total (US$ billion)	2004	428.1	2011	914.8	increasing
Average price level (ppp conversion factors)					
GDP basket of commodities					
ASEAN6: CLMV ratio	2000	1.57	2011	1.56	converging
ASEAN coefficient of variation	2000	0.327	2011	0.251	converging
Consumer basket of commodities					
ASEAN6: CLMV ratio	2000	1.57	2011	1.42	converging
ASEAN coefficient of variation	2000	0.387	2011	0.279	converging
Services trade and investment liberalisation					
Trade in services					
ASEAN total exports (US$ billion)	2005	120.7	2011	260.9	increasing
ASEAN total imports (US$ billion)	2005	143.1	2011	269.1	increasing
Tourist arrivals					
Intra-ASEAN total (millions)	2000	15.9	2011	37.7	increasing

Intra-ASEAN share (%)	2000	40.7	2011	46.5	increasing
Inward FDI					
Intra-ASEAN total (US$ billion)	2000	0.85	2011	26.27	increasing
Intra-ASEAN share (%)	2000	3.9	2011	23.0	increasing
Competitiveness and facilitation of capital flows					
Average cost to trade per container (US$)					
To import	2005	695	2011	742	increasing
To export	2005	795	2011	815	increasing
Effective interest rates					
Deposit (% per year)					
ASEAN6: CLMV (% points)	2000	8.3	2010	8.5	converging
ASEAN coefficient of variation	2000	23.0	2010	3.4	converging
Lending (% per year)					
ASEAN6: CLMV (% points)	2000	1.1	2010	3.1	converging
ASEAN coefficient of variation	2000	2.3	2010	0.9	converging
Domestic credit provision, % of GDP					
From the banking sector					
ASEAN average	2000	55.6	2011	68.0	increasing
ASEAN6: CLMV ratio	2000	9.7	2011	3.3	converging
To the private sector					

Table 5.8 (*cont.*)

Outcome Indicators	Benchmark year	Benchmark value	Latest year	Latest value	Status
ASEAN average	2000	50.7	2011	64.0	increasing
ASEAN6: CLMV ratio	2000	8.8	2011	2.6	converging
Narrowing the development gap					
GDP per capita (ppp$)					
ASEAN average	2000	2882	2011	5581	increasing
ASEAN: CLMV ratio	2000	3.4	2011	2.6	converging
Population with under $1.25 per day (%)					
ASEAN average	2000	32.8	2010	15.3	decreasing
CLMV-ASEAN6 gap (% points)	2000	15.5	2010	1.4	converging
Human development index					
ASEAN average	2005	0.635	2010	0.657	increasing
ASEAN6-CLMV gap (%)	2005	25.0	2010	22.9	converging

Source: ASEAN Secretariat, *ASEAN Brief 2012: Progress Towards the ASEAN Community* (Jakarta: ASEAN Secretariat, 2013).

- Liberalisation of services. Data on intra-ASEAN services trade are not available. However, imports of services have increased rapidly, especially in priority integration sectors such as communications, computer and related information services; travel services; and business services, royalties and licences. Exports of services also increased, reducing the deficit in services trade. Trade in transport services recovered after a substantial decline in 2008 owing to the global financial crisis.
- On people movement via tourism. Intra-ASEAN tourism is becoming more dominant, accounting for a 46.5 per cent share of total ASEAN tourism by 2011.
- Investment liberalisation. Intra-ASEAN inward FDI rose rapidly, particularly since 2009, to reach US$26.3 billion by 2011, a thirtyfold increase since 2000 and accounting for 23 per cent of total FDI inflows into ASEAN.

5.6.2 Competitiveness and facilitation of capital flows

- Competitiveness as measured by costs of trade. The average per-container cost of importing and exporting in ASEAN declined in real terms from 2005 to 2011. However, the cross-country variation in per-container costs remains large, ranging from less than US$400 per container to more than US $2,000. To some extent these cross-country variations may reflect natural geographical differences (with landlocked Laos experiencing higher trading costs).

- Capital flows facilitation. Effective interest rates for lending and deposits continued to show significant variation, although there is a trend towards convergence. On domestic credit provision, while domestic sources of capital appear to have played an increasing role from the mid-2000s, there is still a wide divergence between ASEAN6 and CLMV.

5.6.3 Narrowing the development gap

- While aggregate GDP (in ppp$) grew at an average of 7.7 per cent for ASEAN between 2000 and 2011, it grew faster for CLMV (9.9 per cent) than for ASEAN6 (7.7 per cent), signifying a narrowing of the income gap between the two sub-groups.
- However, the average income gap in absolute terms is still very large, ranging from ppp$2,543 in 2000 to ppp$4,156 in 2011.
- The extent of absolute poverty, as measured by percentage of the population living on less than ppp$1.25 a day, has declined for both ASEAN6 and CLMV, with also a narrowing of the absolute gap.
- The HDI (Human Development Index) for 2005 to 2010 shows CLMV catching up with ASEAN6, but with unequal progress in the economic, health and education indices.

5.7 Realising the AEC objectives by 2015 and beyond

What more needs to be done fully to implement the AEC Blueprint and to achieve the objectives of the AEC?

5.7 AEC OBJECTIVES

5.7.1 Single market and production base

- Utilisation rates of FTA preferences are too low. Some of the problem areas such as ROO and customs procedures are being addressed. Further efforts are needed in simplifying customs procedures and improving certainty of outcomes (including removing corruption at customs). A customs union would remove the problems associated with ROO, but it has problems of its own as outlined in Chapter 6. To improve utilisation of FTA tariff preferences, more publicity blitz and training programmes targeted at SMEs are needed.
- More attention should be focused on removing various other NTBs that impede supply chains such as the administrative regulatory regime and inefficient trade logistics – some of these barriers are indicated in the World Bank's Ease of Doing Business Index and Logistics Performance Index.
- On services sector liberalisation, the various flexibilities and carve-outs need re-examination so that wider and deeper liberalisation can be achieved.
- On investments, countries need to re-examine their exclusion lists and avoid flip-flops in investment policies (particularly on rates of foreign equity and sectors allowed) that create uncertainties for investors. Further, foreign investors often have difficulties accessing various factors of production such as land, finance and skilled workers. Creating special economic zones, such as the highly successful Iskandar region in southern Malaysia, would help create investment-friendly environments for FDI.

- On mobility of ASEAN skilled professionals, some of the domestic regulatory constraints on employment of foreigners should be re-examined, including constitutional constraints on employment of foreigners. ASEAN professional associations should meet regularly to get better acquainted and explore common visions and exchanges.

5.7.2 *Competitive economic region*

- Effective implementation of competition policy would help ensure a level playing field for domestic and foreign investors. The dominant role of SOEs in some countries and sectors should be re-examined.
- ASEAN may also need to explore provisions for government procurement, labour standards and environmental standards, as increasingly found in twenty-first-century agreements, such as in some of the ASEAN+1 agreements and in the TPP agreement under negotiation.
- Corruption is a serious trade and investment barrier in a number of ASEAN countries and needs to be controlled.

5.7.3 *Equitable economic development*

- The implementation record appears excellent, but the strategic actions of SME development and IAI are inadequate to narrow the development gap within and between ASEAN countries. While intra-country inequalities would be mainly the responsibility of national governments, inter-country inequalities could be narrowed with region-wide policies and measures.

- Promoting the accelerated development of CLMV countries is the surest way to narrow the development gap between them and ASEAN6. A major kingpin is for CLMV countries to improve their investment climate and 'ease of doing business', including logistics performance. Current political reforms under way in Myanmar appear to be doing wonders in attracting extra-ASEAN and intra-ASEAN FDI. ASEAN6 countries as well as ASEAN's dialogue and development partners could play their part by encouraging and incentivising their private sectors to invest in CLMV and providing increased economic and technical assistance to CLMV in the form of human resource development; public sector management; agricultural development; urban and transport development; transfers of technology, know-how and development experience; and greater transportation, telecommunications and logistics connectivity through the ASEAN Connectivity Plan and ASEAN Infrastructure Fund. More financial and technical assistance from regional and global institutions such as the Asian Development Bank, World Bank and WTO (aid-for-trade programme) are also called for.

5.7.4 Full integration into the global economy

This pillar achieved a perfect score for implementation. ASEAN has a market of nearly 600 million people, exceeding NAFTA and the EU in population size but only a fraction of their economic size. Hence the need for ASEAN to practise open regionalism and widen its economic networking through various ASEAN-wide FTAs/EPAs and in integrating further into global production networks and supply chains. However, the expansion of extra-ASEAN links through FTAs has also given rise to some concerns over the centrifugal forces weakening ASEAN centrality; the capability of Cambodia, Laos and Myanmar to negotiate on many fronts and to secure the benefits of economic integration; and the emergence of a 'noodle bowl' (diverse time frames for completion, diverse exclusion lists and diverse rules of origin and technical and product standards) that could raise administrative and business transaction costs and discourage utilisation of the tariff preferences.

Chapter 6

Future directions: moving beyond AEC 2015

ASEAN economic cooperation and integration have come a long way. From a set of token cooperative initiatives during its first few decades to the AEC, ASEAN now can boast the most advanced expression of regional economic cooperation and integration of any major region in the developing world.

The progressively outward-oriented nature of the trade and investment regimes of ASEAN member economies is consistent with the direction of the AEC and related initiatives, which stress the need for 'open regionalism' more than most other regional economic groupings. No doubt this reflects the fact that the lion's share of ASEAN's trade and investment interaction is extra-regional. But it is also an expression of ASEAN's development strategy, one that would well be imitated by the many other regional economic groupings sprouting up throughout the world.

Outward orientation has served ASEAN well. It has been one of the fastest growing regions in the world for the past quarter century, with a major downturn only during the AFC of 1997–8. While there is considerable variance in performance across ASEAN countries, per capita income on average has been rising robustly, poverty rates have been falling and social indicators have been improving. Although the USA-originated financial crisis of 2008–9 and the Eurozone Sovereign Debt Crisis have affected ASEAN growth over the past five years owing to their exposure to global markets, liberal trade and investment regimes have allowed them to bounce back quickly, helped in part by buoyant commodity demand by China and India for the natural resources of several ASEAN economies.

We have shown in this study that the AEC has made substantive progress in implementing measures outlined in the AEC Blueprint and in subsequent initiatives such as ASEAN infrastructure connectivity. But much more remains to be done. Indeed, according to the ASEAN Scorecard, the implementation rate has been slowing down rather than rising, as it will need to do to meet the rapidly approaching deadline of 2015. As some of the more difficult issues remain, it will take a good deal of political momentum at the highest levels to ensure a successful outcome.

But, as we have stressed elsewhere (Plummer and Chia 2009), the timing is less significant than the final product, particularly as the original AEC deadline of 2020 was moved forward to 2015. The EU Single Market Programme, dubbed 'EC 1992' owing to the fact that it was intended to be completed at the end of 1992, had only half of its ambitious policy agenda in place by then and just over three-quarters by the end of 1994. But the markets continued to respond positively to the initiative, as they saw so much progress (when there was so much pessimism to start). Today, the Single Market Programme is considered a great success (certainly not to be confused with issues associated with monetary union). Likewise, ASEAN should keep its 'eye on the prize': a single market and production base. It is to be hoped that this can be done by 2015, but what needs to take priority is getting it right rather than getting it done on time.

Indeed, ASEAN economic integration would be best considered a *process*, with the AEC being an important milestone. As noted in this book, much remains to be addressed in creating a truly integrated market. We would like to point out a few challenges as the process continues.

First, it would be difficult to be a truly single market (in the EU sense) in ASEAN unless and until there is complete free movement of goods, that is, without being subject to certification of ROO and NTB. A customs union (CU) has no ROO requirement because its common external tariffs prevent trade deflection, that is, extra-regional goods entering the integrated region through a member country with low external tariffs compared to other members. In reality, there are very few CUs in the global economy, as compared to the proliferation of FTAs, for significant reasons: (a) countries have to pool sovereignty over most (if not all) of their commercial policies; (b) it is never easy to agree on the actual structure of tariffs in the form of a Common External Tariff (CET), particularly in the case of countries with hugely divergent tariff structures to begin with, such as in ASEAN; (c) Article XXIV of the GATT disallows preferential trading arrangements (FTAs and CUs) from raising tariffs against non-members, and infringement would be subject to penalty; and (d) from a practical point of view, CUs are more difficult to devise and implement, forcing a number of additional questions that need to be addressed, such as: who gets the revenue from the CET and how will countries having to lower external tariffs be compensated for the fiscal shock?[1] Hence, a CU requires far more extensive intra-regional negotiations than is the case for an FTA, and this would certainly be complicated in the ASEAN context.

Still, it could be argued that an ASEAN CU would have advantages: most importantly, carrying on with independent commercial policies among ASEAN countries would continue to maintain market segmentation rather than achieve a single market. This was realised in the context of the European Community in developing the Single Market Programme: it had in place a European CET but NTBs such as import quotas were determined at the national level and resulted in considerable price differences across member states. The Single Market Programme integrated all EU commercial policies into a single authority, thereby allowing for the dismantling of border controls and increasing, considerably, market integration. ASEAN would be able to reap many of these benefits as well, making it easier, for example, for regional production networks and eliminating bureaucratic costs such as those associated with ROO.

Creating a CET in ASEAN would be complicated by the considerable dispersion of tariff rates across countries and sectors in ASEAN, with Singapore–Brunei having essentially no tariffs and CLMV countries having relatively high tariffs. Given its role as an entrepôt centre and the significant role of imported inputs in production and consumption, it would mean the loss of Singapore's free port status and greatly disadvantage it against its Hong Kong rival, and the various stakeholders in Singapore would not agree to raising tariffs.

[1] Plummer 2006.

Moreover, raising tariffs would subject Singapore to WTO sanctions. Furthermore, discussion of an ASEAN CU tends to focus only on the differences in tariff regimes between Singapore and the other ASEAN countries. However, where removal of NTBs and harmonising NTMs and having a competitive ASEAN-wide market is concerned, the dichotomy between Singapore and the rest of ASEAN is not so clear cut. What would be the competitive environment with regard to the role of state-owned enterprises and natural resource subsidies? Businesses surveyed are not so much concerned over tariffs inhibiting trade and investment as over obstacles posed by various behind-the-border measures, policies and institutional practices.

One controversial proposal would be to apply an 'ASEAN minus X' formula to an ASEAN CU. That would not appear desirable as it would sideline the role of Singapore in intra-ASEAN trade and intra-ASEAN investments. Further, if the CET is set at an ASEAN 'average' then member countries with average tariff levels below this average may also not agree. The case becomes even more complicated as tariff peaks differ among ASEAN countries for a variety of reasons. In any event an 'ASEAN minus X' formula would create a 'two-tier ASEAN' of a different sort when ASEAN leaders are focused on a unified ASEAN amid concerns of centrifugal forces diluting ASEAN centrality.

Another controversial proposal would be to construct a CET that would converge to zero tariffs over time. It could be implemented at varying speeds, for example, beginning with manufactures and allowing for a certain percentage of excluded products that would eventually be included, more time for implementation for the CLM countries, and so forth. While politically difficult, such a CET would potentially yield strong economic returns, eliminate any negative aspects of preferential trading arrangements and make ASEAN an extremely attractive place for FDI and global and regional production networks.

Second, ASEAN might consider completing the common market by including other aspects that have hitherto been excluded from the AEC. For example, the AEC only envisions the free movement of skilled labour and the freer movement of capital. Integrating the labour and capital markets would be necessary for a common market. Certainly, implementing free movement of unskilled labour will be at least as politically difficult as the creation of a CU, although there could be a caveat that such unskilled labour be required to have secured employment contracts before migrating and migrant workers as well as their home countries must accept that host countries' domestic laws must prevail. The potential economic gains could be significant and it could be considered as a long-term goal. However, a large migrant labour force would raise other political and social issues given the vast differences in land and population sizes and population density among ASEAN countries – for example, between Brunei and Singapore at one extreme and Indonesia and the Philippines at the other extreme. The EU is struggling with this issue today.

Third is the issue of further accessions to ASEAN membership. Timor Leste, which separated from Indonesia in 2002, is already a candidate for accession. While Timor Leste is technically a middle-income economy, its social indicators are on a par with many Least Developed Countries and it has a poor

HDI score. It faces enormous challenges, including increasing employment and diversifying its economy, which is currently completely reliant on oil exports. Another possible candidate for accession is Papua New Guinea, which has been an ASEAN observer since 1976. It is usually referred to as a Pacific Island nation, given its history and culture and participation in various Pacific Islands forums. However, it does share an Island with Indonesia – New Guinea. It is endowed with vast mineral resources but has had major problems in developing other parts of the economy and suffers from pockets of poverty, low formal employment, major corruption problems and serious law and order issues, and its HDI score is even lower than Timor Leste. ASEAN would have to collectively evaluate carefully the political-social-economic benefits and costs of eventual membership of Timor Leste and Papua New Guinea and whether these two countries will enhance ASEAN centrality and economic performance.

Finally, given the rapidly changing regional economic architecture, ASEAN will need to play a more active Asia-wide role to advance its interests. For example, as a concrete manifestation of 'ASEAN centrality', the ASEAN Summit in November 2011 launched the ASEAN Framework on Regional Comprehensive Economic Partnership (RCEP) initiative.[2]

[2] This was in response to the EAFTA-CEPEA dilemma. EAFTA (East Asia Free Trade Area) or ASEAN+3 (involving ASEAN, China, Japan and South Korea) and CEPEA (Comprehensive Economic Partnership for East Asia) or ASEAN+6 (involving ASEAN+3 countries as well as India, Australia and New Zealand) were alternative region-wide FTA initiatives supported respectively by China and Japan, and ASEAN was hard put on which proposal to choose.

The Framework sets out the general principles using as a basis the ASEAN+1 FTAs and EAFTA and CEPEA proposals, and these are as follows.

- **Coverage.** To achieve a comprehensive and mutually beneficial economic partnership agreement, with significant improvement over existing ASEAN FTAs with Dialogue Partners, and provide a basis for addressing future issues.
- **Process.** Agreement can be accomplished sequentially or as a single undertaking or through any other agreed modality.
- **Open accession.** To have an open accession clause to enable participation of any other ASEAN FTA partners (should they not be ready to participate at the outset) as well as any other external economic partners.
- **Economic and technical cooperation.** This will be an integral part of the Agreement to support ASEAN member states and maximise their benefits from implementation of the Agreement.
- **Facilitation.** Agreement shall include practical measures and cooperative efforts to facilitate trade and investment, including reduction of transaction costs for businesses.
- **Economic integration.** Agreement shall contribute to ASEAN economic integration, equitable economic development, and strengthening economic cooperation between ASEAN member states as well as between ASEAN and its partners.
- **Special and differential treatment.** Agreement shall provide for special and differential treatment to ASEAN member states, especially CLMV.

Three working groups on trade in goods, trade in services and investment have been established to define the specific principles and a template under which ASEAN will engage with partners. Negotiations on RCEP began in early 2013 and were expected to conclude in 2015, with the participation of ASEAN10 countries as well as China, Japan, South Korea, India, Australia and New Zealand. It is reported that RCEP will target removal of 95 per cent of tariffs on goods (already committed in several ASEAN+1 FTAs) but it will be harder to achieve sizeable liberalisation in services and in investments.

The timing of the RCEP Framework is to compete with the ongoing Trans-Pacific Partnership (TPP) negotiations involving the USA, Chile, Peru, Australia, New Zealand, as well as the four ASEAN countries of Brunei, Singapore, Malaysia and Vietnam (TPP9), since expanded to TPP12 with the inclusion of Japan, Canada and Mexico (South Korea may also join in the near future). The biggest contrast between RCEP and TPP is expected to be in the scope and content of their agreements. The TPP is modelled after the US template and styled as a 'gold-standard twenty-first century' agreement. It covers not only trade in goods, trade in services and investment but also behind-the-border measures such as IPR, government procurement, competition policy and SOEs, investor-state dispute resolution and labour and environmental standards. RCEP is modelled after the AEC and ASEAN+1 agreements. It covers also trade in goods, trade in services and investment as well as some behind-the-border issues. However, it emphasises flexibility, economic and technical cooperation and special and differential treatment for the less-developed economies and infrastructure development for regional connectivity.

In sum, ASEAN has come a long way, but still has a long way to go, with many exciting prospects as well as challenges that await.

EXECUTIVE SUMMARY

ASEAN economic cooperation and integration have come a long way since the organisation's early days, when co-operation was more political and diplomatic than economic in nature. Beginning with the ASEAN Free Trade Area (AFTA) in 1992, ASEAN economic integration has become increasingly prominent, and in the twenty-first century it represents an integral part of the regional economic landscape.

The ASEAN Economic Community (AEC) initiative, conceived in 2003 and officially launched in 2009, constitutes by far the most ambitious attempt by ASEAN member states to create a 'single market and production base' and envisions arguably the deepest economic integration programme in the developing world. Its goal is to allow free flow of goods, services, foreign direct investment (FDI) and skilled labour and freer flow of capital within the region, to be accomplished by 2015. The AEC is being implemented in the context of a rapidly changing global and regional architecture, with multilateral trade negotiations on hold and 'mega-regional' trade pacts in negotiation, including the Trans-Pacific Partnership (TPP) and the Regional Comprehensive Economic Partnership (RCEP), the latter being a manifestation of 'ASEAN Centrality'. The stakes associated with the successful construction of the AEC are clearly very high for ASEAN and its member states.

The goal of this book is to give a contextual review of ASEAN economic integration in general and the AEC in particular, analyse its economic implications, assess its implementation to date and consider future challenges. Below we summarise some of the major findings.

In terms of the potential economic benefits from the AEC, the literature underscores several key benefits of economic integration, including an enlarged market with economies of scale and scope, improved resource allocation with free movement of factors of production, improved resource pools with inflows of capital and labour, and competition leading to improved efficiency and innovation. In an earlier study (Plummer and Chia 2009), we assessed the benefits of the AEC to various ASEAN stakeholders (government, business, labour, consumers) as stemming from:

- *Benefits from liberalisation of trade in goods and services*, with a single market and production base allowing ASEAN to benefit from economies of scale and efficiency in production network processes, boost competitiveness, strengthen ASEAN institutions and improve the region's socio-economic environment. The elimination of intra-ASEAN tariffs and non-tariff barriers will boost intra-ASEAN trade and in the process have positive effects on economic growth and employment, resulting in more efficient allocation of resources and thus gains in productivity, encouraging foreign and domestic investments, reducing business costs, increasing economic competitiveness, lowering consumer prices and widening consumer choice. Liberalisation of the services sector is particularly important, given its rising contribution to output and employment in the region, relevance to value chains and relatively high status quo barriers. In addition, addressing behind-the-border measures such as those related to competition policy and intellectual property rights (IPR) protection, as well as infrastructure and spatial connectivity, should yield substantial gains.

- *Benefits from liberalisation of investment and skilled labour flows*, with greater FDI inflows bringing in financial resources for fixed investment as well as technological and managerial know-how, participation in regional production networks and global supply chains, resulting in improved efficiency in production and marketing. The ASEAN Comprehensive Investment Area (ACIA), which began implementation in 2012, should lead this process: it is comprised of four components of FDI liberalisation, facilitation, promotion and protection. In addition, skilled labour mobility (including professionals) is essential for effective implementation of services liberalisation and FDI liberalisation as well as for deeper economic integration. A free flow of skilled labour will increase ASEAN's attraction to foreign multinational corporations (MNCs), particularly as it meets their need for intra-corporate transfer of management and technical personnel. The easier movement of ASEAN professionals within the region will facilitate people-to-people contact and enable transfers of know-how, experiences and best practices.

- *Financial and capital market development*, with more efficient markets to finance trade, investment and corporate development in ASEAN countries. Cooperation in ASEAN and in ASEAN+3 (that is, including also China, Japan and South Korea) have resulted in several financial initiatives such as the Chiang Mai Initiative Multilateralised, Asian Bond Market and Regional Surveillance Mechanism.
- *Narrowing the development gap*, with Cambodia, Laos, Myanmar and Vietnam (CLMV) beginning to catch up with the more advanced ASEAN member states. As detailed at length in this study, ASEAN economies are characterised by wide economic diversity in factor endowments, economic structures and levels of economic development. It is generally accepted that a wide development gap would lead to negative spillover effects between rich and poor neighbourhoods as well as hindering consensus building and the speed of progress towards the ASEAN Economic Community. The Initiative for ASEAN Integration (IAI) is the key policy instrument to provide economic and technical development assistance to CLMV countries, embodying also the transfer of know-how, development experience and best practices from the more advanced ASEAN member states. Moreover, regional production networks hold great promise in plugging in CLMV productive factors into the global and regional economies; hence, the anticipated boost to these networks via the AEC should benefit significantly ASEAN's poorest members.

While it is difficult to put numbers to the potential economic effects of the AEC, our earlier study used a Computable General Equilibrium (CGE) model to gauge the effects assuming complete elimination of tariffs and non-tariff barriers (NTBs), liberalisation of five service sectors, AEC-induced changes in FDI and a 5 per cent reduction in trade costs. Despite the fact that some of the most important benefits of the AEC are not included in the simulated scenarios (for example, competition policy, greater IPR protection, financial cooperation, other behind-the-border measures), the study estimates that the increase in economic welfare should be 5.3 per cent or US$69 billion relative to the baseline, that is, more than six times the effect estimated for completing AFTA. All ASEAN countries benefit.

Hence, the potential gains are large. Nevertheless, implementation of such an ambitious programme in the context of such a diverse region is difficult. The 'ASEAN Scorecard', an implementation tracking mechanism undertaken by the ASEAN Secretariat, attempts to gauge annual progress in meeting the exigencies of the AEC Blueprint. In essence, ASEAN countries appear to have thus far fully implemented commitments related to freer flow of capital (except Myanmar), free flow of skilled labour, priority integration sectors, competition policy, minerals, information and communication technology (ICT), taxation (except Cambodia) and e-commerce. Moreover, all ASEAN countries appear to have more than half implemented free flow of goods, free flow of services, free flow of investments, food-agriculture-forestry, consumer protection, transport, energy, IAI and external economic relations. However, the compliance record is mixed. Much remains to be done if the AEC is to be completed on schedule. Indeed, the implementation rate has been slowing down rather than rising as it will need to do to meet the rapidly approaching deadline of 2015. As some of the more difficult issues remain, it will take a good deal of political momentum at the highest levels to ensure a successful outcome.

Still, the timing is less significant than the final product. The EU Single Market Programme, dubbed 'EC 1992' owing to the fact that it was intended to be completed at the end of 1992, had only half of its ambitious policy agenda in place by then and just over three-quarters by the end of 1994. But the markets continued to respond positively to the initiative, as they saw so much progress (when there was so much pessimism to start). Today, the Single Market Programme is considered a great success (certainly not to be confused with issues associated with monetary union). Likewise, ASEAN should keep its 'eye on the prize': a single market and production base. Hopefully this can be done by 2015, but what needs to take priority is getting it right rather than getting it done on time.

In sum, ASEAN economic cooperation and integration have come a long way. From a set of token cooperative initiatives during its first few decades to a 'single market and production base' in the form of the AEC, ASEAN now can boast an increasingly integrated region with a clear plan for deepening integration in the future. The progressively outward-oriented nature of the trade and investment regimes of ASEAN member economies is consistent with the direction of the AEC and related initiatives, which stress the need for 'open regionalism' more than most other regional economic groupings. No doubt this reflects the fact that the lion's share of ASEAN's trade and investment interaction is extra-regional. But it also is an expression of ASEAN's development strategy, one that could well be imitated by the many other regional economic groupings sprouting up throughout the world.

Outward orientation has served ASEAN well. It has been one of the fastest growing regions in the world for the past quarter century, with a major downturn only during the Asian Financial Crisis of 1997–8. While there is considerable variance in performance across ASEAN countries, per capita income on average has been rising robustly, poverty rates have been falling and social indicators have been improving. Although the USA-originated financial crisis of 2008–9 and the Eurozone Sovereign Debt Crisis affected ASEAN growth significantly over the past five years owing to their exposure to global markets, liberal trade and investment regimes have allowed them to bounce back quickly, helped in part by buoyant commodity demand (until recently) by China and India for the resource-rich ASEAN economies.

Finally, given the rapidly changing regional economic architecture, ASEAN will need to play an active, contributing role to advance its interests. ASEAN leaders realise this. For example, in November 2012 ASEAN and six of its FTA partners launched the RCEP initiative, which is to create a 'flexible' FTA; ongoing negotiations are expected to be concluded in 2015. With some ASEAN members being part of the ongoing TPP negotiations while others are not, the RCEP will serve to unite ASEAN under the Asian-FTA track while allowing the more ambitious economies to participate in the TPP as well.

In sum, ASEAN has come a long way, but still has a long way to go, with many exciting prospects as well as challenges that await.

BIBLIOGRAPHY

Akrasanee, Narongchai (2000) 'ASEAN in the Past Thirty-three Years: Lessons for Economic Cooperation', in Simon Tay, J. Estanisllao and H. Soesastro (eds), *A New ASEAN in a New Millennium*, Jakarta: Centre for Strategic and International Studies.

ASEAN Secretariat (2008) *The ASEAN Economic Community Blueprint*. Jakarta: ASEAN Secretariat.

(2009) *Roadmap for an ASEAN Community 2009–2015*. Jakarta: ASEAN Secretariat.

(2012a) *ASEAN Economic Community Handbook for Business 2012*. Jakarta: ASEAN Secretariat.

(2012b) *ASEAN Economic Community Scorecard: Charting Progress Towards Regional Economic Integration*. Jakarta: ASEAN Secretariat.

(2013a) *ASEAN Brief 2012: Progress Towards the ASEAN Community*. Jakarta: ASEAN Secretariat.

(2013b) *ASEAN Community Progress Monitoring System: Full Report 2012*. Jakarta: ASEAN Secretariat.

(2013c) *ASEAN Statistical Yearbook 2012*. Jakarta: ASEAN Secretariat.

Asian Development Bank (2008) *Emerging Asian Regionalism*. Manila: Asian Development Bank.

(2012) *Asian Development Outlook 2012*. Manila: Asian Development Bank.

Athukorala, Prema-Chandra (2010) 'Production Networks and Trade Patterns in East Asia: Regionalization or Globalization?', *Asian*

Development Bank Working Paper Series on Regional Economic Integration, No. 56. Manila: Asian Development Bank.

Baer, Werner (1972) 'Import Substitution and Industrialisation in Latin America: Experiences and Interpretations', *Latin American Research Review* 7.1: 95–122.

Chayodom, S. and K. Cheewatratoolpong (2012) 'The Impact of the AEC on ASEAN Production Networks', background for the ASEAN 2030 study, Asian Development Bank Institute mimeo.

Chia, Siow Yue (2011a) 'Association of Southeast Asian Nations Economic Integration: Developments and Challenges', *Asian Economic Policy Review* 6.1: 43–63.

(2011b) 'Free Flow of Skilled Labor in the ASEAN Economic Community', in Shujiro Urata and Misa Okabe (eds.), *Toward a Competitive ASEAN Single Market: Sectoral Analysis* (Project Report 2010–13). Jakarta: Economic Research Institute for ASEAN and East Asia: 205–79, available at: www.eria.org/publications/research_project_reports/images/pdf/y2010/no3/Chapter4.pdf.

(2011c) 'Singapore', in Masahiro Kawai and Ganeshan Wignaraja (eds.), *Asia's Free Trade Agreements: How is Business Responding?* Cheltenham: Edward Elgar.

(2013a) *The ASEAN Economic Community: Progress, Challenges and Prospects*, Asian Development Bank Working Paper, No. 440. Tokyo: Asian Development Bank.

(2013b) 'The Emerging Regional Economic Integration Architecture in East Asia', *Asian Economic Papers*, 12.1: 1–37.

Dennis, D. J. and Z. A. Yusof (2003) 'Developing Indicators of ASEAN Integration: A Preliminary Survey for a Roadmap', Final Report on Regional Economic Policy Support Facility Project 02/001, mimeo.

Feridhanusetyawan, Tubagus (2005) 'Preferential Trade Agreements in the Asia-Pacific Region', *IMF* Working Paper WP/05/149. Washington, DC: International Monetary Fund.

Hew, Denis (ed.) (2007) *Brick by Brick: The Building of an ASEAN Economic Community*. Singapore: Institute of Southeast Asian Studies.

Kawai, Masahiro and Ganeshan Wignaraja (eds.) (2011) *Asia's Free Trade Agreements: How is Business Responding?* Cheltenham: Edward Elgar.

Little, Ian, Tibor Scitovsky and Maurice Scott (1970) *Industry and Trade in Some Developing Countries: A Comparative Study*. New York: Oxford University Press.

Nikomborirak, Deunden and S. Jitdumrong (2013) 'An Assessment of the Implementation of AEC Service Liberalisation Milestones', in S. B. Das (ed.), *ASEAN Economic Community Scorecard: Performance and Perception*. Singapore: Institute of Southeast Asian Studies.

Petri, Peter A., Michael G. Plummer and Fan Zhai (2012) 'The Economic Impact of the ASEAN Economic Community: An Applied General Equilibrium Approach', *Asian Economic Journal* 26.2: 93–118.

Plummer, Michael G. (2006) 'Towards Win-Win Regionalism in Asia: Issues and Challenges in Forming Efficient Trade Agreements', Asian Development Bank Working Paper Series on Regional Economic Integration, No. 5. Manila: Asian Development Bank.

Plummer, Michael G. and Siow Yue Chia (eds.) (2009) *Realizing the ASEAN Economic Community: A Comprehensive Assessment*. Singapore: Institute of Southeast Asian Studies.

Prasad, Eswar, M. Ayhan Kose, Kenneth S. Rogoff and Shang-Jin Wei (2006) 'Financial Globalization: A Reappraisal', National Bureau of Economic Research Working Papers, 12484. Cambridge, MA: National Bureau of Economic Research.

Severino, Roldofo C. (2006) *Southeast Asia in Search of an ASEAN Community: Insights from the Former ASEAN Secretary-General*. Singapore: Institute of Southeast Asian Studies.

Vo Tri, Thanh (2013) '*Effectiveness of Initiative for ASEAN Integration*', in S. B. Das (ed.), *ASEAN Economic Community Scoreboard: Performance and Perception*. Singapore: Institute of Southeast Asian Studies.

United Nations Industrial Development Organization (UNIDO) (1986) *Regional Industrial Cooperation: Experiences and Perspectives of ASEAN and the Andean Pact*. Vienna: United Nations Industrial Development Organization.

World Bank (2010) *Connecting to Compete: Trade Logistics in the Global Economy*. Washington, DC: World Bank.

(2013) *Doing Business 2014: Understanding Regulations for Small and Medium-Size Enterprises*. Washington, DC: World Bank.

INDEX

INDEX

INDEX